THE
WOODEN
BREEKS

Glen Berger

BROADWAY PLAY PUBLISHING INC
224 E 62nd St, NY NY 10065
212 772-8334 fax 212 772-8358
BroadwayPlayPubl.com

First printing: February 2014
I S B N: 978-0-88145-457-4

Book design: Marie Donovan
Typographic controls & page make-up: Adobe InDesign
Typeface: Palatino
Printed and bound in the U S A

ABOUT THE AUTHOR

Glen Berger's plays include UNDERNEATH THE LINTEL (more than 450 performances off Broadway; several Best Play awards; more than 200 productions in the United States; translated into eight languages), O LOVELY GLOWWORM (2005 Portland Drammy Award for Best Script), and GREAT MEN OF SCIENCE, NOS. 21 & 22 (1998 Ovation Award and L.A. Weekly Award for Best Play).

His television credits include two Emmy Awards (twelve total nominations) and more than 150 episodes for children's series, including *Arthur* (P B S), *Peep* (Discovery/The Learning Channel), *Big and Small* (B B C), and *Fetch* (P B S), for which he was head writer for all five of its seasons. Berger was the co-bookwriter for SPIDER-MAN TURN OFF THE DARK on Broadway, directed by Julie Taymor, with music by Bono and Edge of U2. He wrote a book of that experience—*Song of Spider-Man*—which was published by Simon & Schuster in 2013. He is an alumnus of New Dramatists.

CHARACTERS & SETTING

Tom "Chimney" Bosch, *The Tinker*

Wicker Grigs, *The Orphan. Nine or Tenish years old*

Enry Leap, *The Vicar*

Toom the Stoup, *The Gravedigger*

Mrs (Fanny) Nelles, *The Publichouse Proprietoress*

Armitage Shanks, *The Swain*

Tricity Tiara, *The Laundry Maid*

Jarl van Hoother, *The Lighthouse Keeper. Attractive, dashing even, with an intellectual, owlish intensity, i.e., never "prissy" or florid. Lines delivered quickly and crisply.*

Hetty Grigs/Anna Livia Spoon, *played by the same actress*

Setting: The play opens some time in latter 19th century, Scotland. In Bosch's tale, however, Brood is a fairy-tale town on an unspecified British coast. Don't (obviously) let accents impede intelligibility or conveyance of emotional truth. (And Hoother's voice should probably be "accentless," i.e., a regionless American accent is appropriate for an American production)

Set: The bell device could be quite unnecessarily elaborate, rather than the mostly staid models that actually existed, though I'm not sure if I care. A good model for the lighthouse (And bell device [and whole tone of the play]), is the original Eddystone lighthouse designed in 1699 by Winstanley. Other visual inspirations include 17th century naturalist engravings, Victorian illustrations of Mother Goose, *the paintings of Joseph Wright of Derby (for lighting), and, for Armitage and Tricity—Victorian Pastoral Paintings (e.g.* The Hireling Shepherd*). Also, elemental qualities—such as tobacco, dung, peat, hay, and smoke—would be nice, for the nose.*

Music: The tone of the play was inspired primarily by the 19th century Geneva Titan. It was a music box connected to a pump organ, that played lovely stumbling, plinking, wheezing waltzes in particular. HOOTHER's *environment should, (at least at the top), feel bright, airy, clean, crisp, and expressing a glorious world of sense and logic that we would all love to reside in. 18th century harpsichord suggested— which can dismantle as the play proceeds. In contrast, Brood is muck, earth. A bagpipe makes sense—a bleating sheep's bladder—as well as a huffing accordion.*

A Last Note: Though broods (and Brood) are generally acknowledged as miserable places to dwell, broods (and Brood) are also, perversely, very inviting. Cozy. Familiar. Hence, any production should avoid the temptation to become over-adorned, or emphasize the claustrophobic or fantastical. I can't stress this enough. Find the beating heart and hew closely to it. Ground the play, make emotional truth paramount, keep the storytelling nimble and clear. The humor will come out better this way too.

INTRODUCTION
AND CURSORY SYNOPSIS

In 19th century Britain, panic swept the land when coffins randomly unearthed were found to contain scratchmarks on the inside of the lid. Apparently people were being mistakenly pronounced dead when in fact they were merely comatose, and, subsequently, buried alive. ("Breeks" is Scots dialect for breeches, and "the wooden breeks" literally, "the wooden pants" the vernacular for a coffin.) To allay the fears of the populace, companies began producing bell devices. Such a device could sit on top of your grave, with a cord that ran down a tube through the ground, and into your coffin. If you found yourself alive in your coffin, you could pull the cord, which triggered the bell, which alerted the town to come and unearth you. However, a worm, or the wind, or the shifting of bones would often trigger the cord, and there was more than one incident of a crowd running to unearth a resuscitated corpse only to be met with the more-than-disheartening sight of a loved one in an advanced state of putrefaction. It is within this world of desperate hope and mourning that our story unfolds.

THE WOODEN BREEKS begins outside the town of Clekan-wittit, latter nineteenth century. A tinker, Tom "Chimney" Bosch, is putting out the remains of a fire in his firepit while brooding about a woman he once madly loved named Hetty. Hetty had surprised the courting Bosch by suddenly marrying a worthless sailor. She became pregnant, her husband abandoned her, and Bosch proposed to her soon after the birth of her bairn, Wicker. Hetty accepted, but left for "a brief but unavoidable errand," before the wedding, promising she'd return before the tinker's fire currently flickering in the firepit had died. However, she never did return. Nine years pass, with Bosch feeding his fire in the increasingly bleak hope that Hetty will make good her promise and return before his "little fire" dies out, suspecting all the while that she simply abandoned her son and himself. Bosch, despising Wicker and assuming no responsibility over the years in the raising of him, has, nevertheless, on occasion, indulged the urchin and narrated yet another chapter in an interminable and wholly fictional saga of where Hetty Grigs is now, and why it is taking her so damned long to return (adventures ranging from "being marauded by pirates" to "long line at the shops"). Bosch claims his inspiration for these chapters comes from "the little tinker's fire" itself.

However, when the play opens, we find Bosch putting out the fire. He has resolved once and for bloody all to leave this corner of the world (and Wicker) behind. Before he manages to leave however, a cow-urine-soaked Wicker appears. Wicker, desperate to keep Bosch from leaving, discovers one last unextinguished (And seemingly unextinguishable) ember in the firepit. Although Bosch can't stand the sight of this homeless urchin, he relents to Wicker's pleadings and agrees to use the ember to narrate one last confounded chapter of the endless tale, adding that when the ember dies, he's abandoning the orphaned boy forever.

As Bosch begins to narrate, the ember in the firepit rises to become the light of a lighthouse. Bosch has placed Wicker and himself in Brood, a sort of miserable

and famine-plagued Brigadoon. In Brood, we find Jarl
van Hoother, the lighthouse keeper, who has never
left the lighthouse—not once in his life—his only
contact with the outside world being appendices to
the Ferguson and Ives Natural Science Encyclopaedia
that are delivered through his mailslot; Armitage
Shanks and Tricity Tiara, the town lovers, who have
vowed never to marry, for "marriage is the enemy
of true love"; Mrs Nelles, who has been in mourning
over the death of her daughter for innumerable years
now, and, with unintentioned cruelty, has kept the
single public house of Brood shut all the while, thus
depriving the town of drink; Enry Leap, the Vicar,
nursing a secret and painful long-standing love for
Mrs Nelles and her whiskey; Toom the Stoup, the
occasionally graverobbing gravedigger; and Wicker
Grigs, whom Bosch, spitefully, has placed in the tale
as a much-abused orphan who delivers the post. Bosch
intends the chapter to be as dull, as abusive-to-Wicker,
and as Hetty-less as he can, so that Wicker will give up
and let Bosch abandon the story (and Wicker). Wicker,
however, is just as determined to keep Bosch from
leaving, and insists that the story has to continue until
the ember (now the lighthouse light) dies, just as Bosch
had promised.

Bosch summons a salesman to help him get into the
impenetrable lighthouse and snuff the flame, but, to
Bosch's surprise, the salesman to arrive is a woman—
Anna Livia Spoon—who bears an uncanny, suspicious
resemblance to Hetty Grigs. She has come selling bell
devices, and has just one more to sell to make her
quota. She isn't in town long before all the inhabitants
have been affected by her singular presence. However,
due perhaps to the town's crushing proverty, she is
unable to sell her last device. By the end of Act One,
she has died under curious circumstances, and her last

bell device is erected over her own grave. But is she really dead? Is that bell ever going to ring? What brings us to Brood? What keeps us in Brood? And how do we escape from that cursed place?

And mind you, "to brood" means not only "to mull darkly over events long past" but also "to await for new life to hatch."

ACT ONE

*(The tinker, TOM "CHIMNEY" BOSCH sits in front of a firepit, where a small fire burns. Littering the stage are Implements of BOSCH's trade, and also an impressive number of scuffed books [Literature, science, etc.], a battered accordion, portable cooking pot, etc. —items to be used as props by characters for the rest of the play. [**Optional: Begin with BOSCH singing a song—see end of script**])*

BOSCH: There once was a storyteller held captive by a nefarious magical fire. Don't you doubt it...twas magical...and twas nefarious. For no matter how hard the storyteller tried, he couldn't leave it, he couldn't let the fire die even if it meant dying himself. Twas grisly. But this was just the beginning of the fire's awful magic. For the fettered storyteller couldn't even avert his eyes from the blaze once he discovered all he had to do was get himself foaming drunk—that was step one—then peer deep into an ember of the fire...and a story would appear to him. Or to be more accurate, another chapter of the same story. Or to be more accurate still, another interminable chapter of the dullest most torturing choking-noise-of-a-story ever concocted. Why was the storyteller driven to seek out these soul-destroying chapters? Cause twas a twinkly magical arsehole of a fire. And as if this whole scene wasn't gruesome enough, every bloody evening, be-spelled, compelled, our storyteller would shout to the world "Let's have us a recap!," *(Beside himself—)* a

RECAP!, and against his will, he would harass himself once more with the wretchedest chapter of them all....Chapter One. Chapter One! "Once upon a time, a cheery, book-smart, and brainless Tinker arrived in a little hamlet called Clekan-wittit and wouldn't have stayed more than a day. If he hadn't gone and encountered a woman.

(HETTY GRIGS *appears, whistling an air [badly], and beginning to examine/gather some of* BOSCH's *gear/books/ concertina*)

BOSCH: *(Brooding, still narrating)* Hetty Grigs. And blast her to smithereens." *(To* HETTY*)* Hey you, yes, can you be a nuisance somewhere else perhaps. Neptune, perhaps.

HETTY: Is that how you talk to all the fetching young maidens?

BOSCH: If it's fetching you're doing, try that stick over there instead of my expensive tongs.

HETTY: *(Dubious)* Expensive?

BOSCH: Aye, put that down and run along home.

HETTY: *(Surveying disapprovingly)* You've strewn yourself all along the road.

BOSCH: Well what else is a poor tinker to do?

HETTY: *(Idly perusing* BOSCH's *books)* I'm sure you're as intelligent as anyone else, you just don't consider how you're affecting others. *(Waggling finger)* Change, I say, or you'll always be a poor thinker.

BOSCH: Eh? *(Clarifying)* I'm a poor tinker.

HETTY: Aye, but pronounce it proper—it's "thinker."

BOSCH: *(Irascibly)* Not when it's "tinker"!

HETTY: You have nothing to recommend yourself, do you.

BOSCH: I serve as I can, your Majesty.

HETTY: Oh, so you've heard I'm from royalty.

BOSCH: The royal pain in the arse, I imagine.

HETTY: Well I have nothing for you to tinker with, sir.

BOSCH: Perfect in every way are you?

HETTY: Oh, do you mend spoons? I have a spoon—

BOSCH: —and it's wanting a firm hand to put it right?

HETTY: If that's your professional assessment.

BOSCH: *(Narrating)* More glabber—

HETTY: —buckets of it—

BOSCH: —and in the middle of it…

(Long pause)

HETTY: What.

BOSCH: What indeed.

HETTY: …and then a little more gandying,

BOSCH: and then…

HETTY: …she took the tinker home…

BOSCH: …and he mended her spoon.

HETTY: Aye, scoured her oven too.

BOSCH: Swept her chimney with his stiff brush—

HETTY: Then thrust his poker in her ingle and stirred it round, and all that night—

BOSCH: That Fat Flirt… That's all he did. *(Indignant)* Bloody Housework! *(Melting)* But that grin— *(Dispelling her)* NO! *(With back to audience, unbuttons his fly, a stream of urine extinguishes the coals as—)* The tinker, pushed one night beyond the beyont by this antique rigmarole…murdered the magical fire…aye!…. …with his own magical urine. Released from the spell, he called out— "See you in Hell, Hetty Grigs…we're off!" And he was off—

(But just as he's about to exit, we hear from offstage—)

WICKER: Mister Bosch!

BOSCH: *(Beyond frustration)* No!

(WICKER GRIGS enters, sopping wet, nose running, bawling his eyes out)

WICKER: Mister Bosch—

BOSCH: He left already!

WICKER: *(In terrible tears)* They pushed me in the addle!

BOSCH: *(Not listening or caring)* Fine.

WICKER: They watched the cow streel where other cows streeled and it made a puddle…

(WICKER's tears, trembling, and hyperventilation momentarily pauses his narrative)

BOSCH: *(Impatiently)* Yes?

WICKER: …and then they pushed me in it.

BOSCH: *(Making to go)* Well I'm glad to see you're making friends.

WICKER: *(Grabbing onto BOSCH)* I don't have any friends. I don't have anyone. Except you.

BOSCH: Get off me! I don't even know your name!

WICKER: *(Panicked)* It's Wicker Grigs!

BOSCH: Nope. Never heard of it.

WICKER: *(Panicked)* You were going to marry me moother!

BOSCH: Marry your mother?! If anyone tells you that, they're lying! Hetty Grigs was the most conniving—

WICKER: She was nice!

BOSCH: You hardly saw her before she abandoned you.

WICKER: *(Taking out a small tintype)* I have a picture.

BOSCH: Let me see that.

(As BOSCH *stares at tintype—)*

WICKER: And she didn't abandon me. She just got held up is all!

BOSCH: *(Still staring at picture)* At an extremely busy sheep crossing.

WICKER: Maybe she got in an accident!

BOSCH: *(Turning back, savagely)* You were an accident. No one wanted you here, not your shank of a father, not your mother, No one!

(Beat. BOSCH *throws down tintype, makes to leave.* WICKER, *sniffling, picks up tintype)*

WICKER: *(Whispered slowly, fiercely, with tears—)* …I didn't want to be here either…I doon't want to be alive…I hate it….

*(*BOSCH *looks at urine-drenched* WICKER *with begrudging compassion.)*

BOSCH: *(Angrily)* …stop dripping….

WICKER: *(Pathetic)* I can't stop dripping. But maybe if I sat by your magical fire—

BOSCH: There's no fire.

WICKER: *(Not absorbing info)* —and listen to another chapter about mother. And why she's taking so long to come back—

BOSCH: The story's done.

WICKER: It can't be done—you just need to stare into the fire and—

*(*BOSCH *grabs* WICKER *savagely by the collar and drags him to the firepit)*

BOSCH: AND DO YOU SEE ANY FIRE!? EH?! A
single ember and I'd tell you more story. But it's dead,
(Leaving) so so long Mister Canker, write me never.

(WICKER grabs BOSCH's trouser leg with all his might)

WICKER: You can't go!

BOSCH: I'll bash your head in if you rip these trousers!

WICKER: But I've no place to go!

BOSCH: The Crumps!

WICKER: They chooked me out.

BOSCH: The Pallivers then.

WICKER: Chooked me out!

BOSCH: Christ in Heaven, can't you keep yourself
indoors for half an hour?!

WICKER: Do you know where I doos my sleeping now?

BOSCH: I'm not interested.

WICKER: I doos my—

BOSCH: I'm not interested!

WICKER: I joost want—

BOSCH: I know what you want. Goodbye.

*(BOSCH shoves WICKER and makes to exit, but WICKER,
peering into ashes—)*

WICKER: *(Eyes widening)* …Mister Bosch… *(Pointing
excitedly)* Mister Bosch! A blink! In the pit!

*(As WICKER grabs BOSCH's coattails, trying to drag him
back—)*

BOSCH: *(Overlapping)* I told you it's dead—

WICKER: *(Showing BOSCH—)* Look—I swear!

BOSCH: Well what of it.

WICKER: That's more story then!

BOSCH: Eh? *(Beat, then realizes—)* Oh no you don't.

WICKER: You said "a single ember—"

(BOSCH smothers the ember with his foot—)

BOSCH: There.

WICKER: Look! It's still there!

(BOSCH steps into the pit, jumps and shuffles about violently as—)

BOSCH: Show me the addle, and I'll drown you in it! *(Getting out of pit)* There. No story.

WICKER: But Mister Bosch! Look! It's still blinking!

BOSCH: *(And as he, agape, stares disbelieving into the pit—)* It's not possible…

WICKER: Please, Mister Bosch!…you promised……

(Pause. BOSCH looks at pathetic dripping creature in front of him.)

BOSCH: Another chapter is it?

WICKER: Yes please. With mother in it. Lots of extra mother in it please.

BOSCH: *(Rage and resignation)* Fine. But you listen to me, you miserable smolt… The moment that bloody ember goes out, I'm done, your wretched face is out of my life for good. Understood?!

(WICKER nods eagerly. BOSCH stomps on the ember again, to no avail—)

BOSCH: *(Stomping)* Bloody Hell…How do I get this blinter to die!

WICKER: Tis a magical fire—you've said it yourself!

BOSCH: I was being wry!

(BOSCH tries smothering it some more as—)

WICKER: *(Shrugging simply)* Well, that's a magical blink that is.

BOSCH: *(With derision—)* A blink…. *(Now growing thoughtful as he stares at blinking ember, and begins to see a story)* …A blink…blink…

(The ember blinking in the firepit now rises magically and becomes the blinking light of a lighthouse. Critical that audience understands that the ember in the firepit and the ember in the lighthouse are one and the same. Underneath the lighthouse blink sits JARL VAN HOOTHER, *the lighthouse keeper, cup of tea next to him, studying his books by a candle)*

BOSCH: *(Narrating)* …it isn't an ember at all, but a lighthouse—

HOOTHER: *(Reading)* —"blink."

BOSCH: *(Peering up at lighthouse)* …blink…he thinks and thinks…squinting by the glim…blink….

HOOTHER: *(Studying jauntily)* Blink…the blink of the great grey owl, strix nebulosa, compare with the barn owl, tyto alba, and its blink of eye; one blink of owl exposited in sixteen diagrams by Smollet— *(Sips loudly)* Good Tea, This. *(Immediately resumes studying)* —by Smollet, with commentary by Chalmers, aided by Nollet…

BOSCH: *(Now becoming clearer with his story)* High up in his lighthouse, Jarl van Hoother sits snug as can be There with his view and his books and his tea

HOOTHER: His tea and his view and incomparable books—

BOSCH: Out the window for ships he occasionally looks—

HOOTHER: But a mast or a sail he never did see

BOSCH: So life was a study in Study and Tea.

WICKER: It must be very noof and tosie up there.

BOSCH: The noofest and tosiest—

WICKER: And is that where moother is?

BOSCH: Nay.

WICKER: Has Hoother seen her then and—

BOSCH: *(Clearer in story)* Nay, he's never seen anyone. He's never left the lighthouse.

WICKER: Never?

BOSCH: Not a once. He's never been outside.

WICKER: Never?

BOSCH: What did I just say! He's Never Been Outside!

WICKER: But—

BOSCH: *(More clear in his story)* His parents vanished when he was a wee wint of a thing and he up-grew in that lamphouse all alone, charged with one solemn duty—

HOOTHER: Keep the flame alive!

BOSCH: His only contact with the outside world being the very particular books that come through his mailslot—

HOOTHER: *(Closes book with finality)* Done. Be sure of it. Done?…Done. Last figure and last word on last page of Appendix 63 stroke J of volume 83 of folio 21 of the Ferguson and Ives Natural Science Illustrated Compendium. Well done. *(Sips tea and approves)* Very nice. *(Sets off foghorn and approves)* Very nice. Well Jarl van Hoother, all is right, and no need to stir, oh no—for soon in the ear we'll hear the slap of the flap of the mailslot below, and through it, what, *(With great satisfaction)* …but another appendix of the Ferguson and Ives… Good…. *(Checking lighthouse light above him—)* Blink….

BOSCH: …blink…

WICKER: And what about moother?

(Ignoring WICKER, BOSCH continues to narrate, now focused entirely on story. Low drone of music underneath—)

BOSCH: …Near the Isle of Mull, and south of Muck, sits a lighthouse in a Town awash in woe, doused in murk, rattled by howling winds and haggling weather—

WICKER: Is it far from Clekan-wittit then?

BOSCH: When were we ever in Clekan-wittit? This is where we are, and this is where we've been. In the wretchedest place on earth— The village of Brood!

(A bagpipe drones and lights up on Brood, where a scowling moon sets, and an ambivalent sun rises. Note: For the rest of the play BOSCH possesses only a scrap of control and foreknowledge of the story, discovering and puzzling out the events and inhabitants of the town as they are revealed.)

HOOTHER: *(Jauntily—and never referencing the outside, but rather, only his books—)* While we await our new appendix, we'll review: The world in a word… "Glorious." The sun rises, see Rumphius, folio 51, and the cock, gallus domesticus, seeing Rumphius, crows.

(And we hear cocks crow, dogs bark, kirk bells tong, and cows low)

BOSCH: Brood. The dogs are lame, the sheep have Bott's, yet still they bark and bleat to greet the day.

HOOTHER: As defined by Nollet and Davies, morning has arrived.

BOSCH: And all in the town of Brood habble to life once more, including a small round pellet of dung named Wicker Grigs, the town's postal bairn. *(Handing WICKER a cap)* Here's your cap—

WICKER: But—

(Launching WICKER *off with a kick to the backside)*

BOSCH: Now get on with you—there's post to deliver!

*(*WICKER *runs off, and* BOSCH *sees—)*

BOSCH: And on the steps of the empty kirk, that would be Vicar Enry Leap at morning prayer—

(Lights up on ENRY LEAP *and* TOOM THE STOUP*)*

LEAP: Dear Lord, look down on your little town of Brood and see it famine-plagued and worse—

TOOM: *(Muttering)* Worse is right—we've got to listen to you.

LEAP: *(Ignoring* TOOM*)* The very air is haggard and waesome—

TOOM: And it's all coming from your gob.

LEAP: *(Ignoring again)* They say, O Lord, You give crumbs to the Ravens when they cry… Where…where, O Lord, are our crumbs?

TOOM: He gives them to ravens, not Great Tits.

LEAP: *(Erupting)* Will you keep quiet?! Holy Christ— Every morning it's the same!

TOOM: It's the same alright.

BOSCH: *(Narrating)* And here comes Wicker Grigs full-tilt at postal errands—

*(*WICKER *is rubbing arm, bottom, or other place where baisting took place)*

WICKER: I just got a baisting for not delivering the post yester-morn!

*(*WICKER *resumes running.)*

LEAP: *(Calling out)* Deliver the post on time today lad!

BOSCH: *(Calling out, with relish)* Or you'll get the lashing of your life! *(Resuming narration)* Off scambles the orphan on a postal route of brambles, dung, japes, jeerings and Toom the Stoup, the gravedigger, who once killed a baby for the bit of coral round its neck—

TOOM: T'isn't true, you bastard!

BOSCH: And what of those other rumors—that you rob from the graves in addition to digging them?

TOOM: T'isn't true! It's shocking what townsfolk will say. If this jacket seems small, tis only cause I've grown, and this dainty cameo brooch… *(Ridiculously long pause 8 seconds minimum as he thinks, and then—)* … twas a gift. *(Spying WICKER)* And where are you off to, Master Grigs?

(WICKER is holding a stack of books and a parcel in brown paper—NELLES' cyanide)

WICKER: *(Trembling with fear of TOOM)* I wasn't!

TOOM: *(Blocking WICKER's way, and mocking his voice)* "Jarl van Hoother, your books have arrived."

WICKER: *(Dutifully)* Appendixes. From Ferguson and Ives.

TOOM: *(Brandishing knife)* Shall we have a look at your appendix, Wick?

WICKER: Please sir, I've noothing —

TOOM: *(Fishing in pocket)* What's in your pocket then—

WICKER: Just my moother!—

TOOM: Your mother? *(Snatching tintype)* Hetty Grigs, am I right?… *(With a sleight of hand he makes it disappear)* Abandoned you again!

WICKER: *(Alarmed)* Where'd she go?!

TOOM: Aye, where'd she go, Wick, after you wurbled out of her? Took one look at you, up-threw, then legged it, didn't she!

WICKER: She's coming back!

TOOM: She's shoved under the ground somewhere!

WICKER: She isn't!

TOOM: (*Demonstrating—as if to urinate*)
Sure—Some graiper's streeling on her gravestone as
we speak.

WICKER: T'isn't true!

TOOM: (*Grabbing* WICKER) And I promise you this,
billy-bentie—if you don't get us a crust to eat, and
soon, it'll be my cack on your own gravestone, and
quick enough.

(*And* TOOM *shoves* WICKER *to the ground.*)

BOSCH: And on with his errands—

WICKER: —To the stream for to get the laundry, but
first deliver the rat poison to Mrs Nelles —do you have
a biscuit in your cupboard, Mrs Nelles?

(WICKER *slides a package under or through a door as lights
up [dim] on* MRS NELLES *in the publichouse. She is dressed
in Victorian mourning black.* WICKER *remains outside the
publichouse door.*)

BOSCH: Alas, the cupboard is bare, there in the public
house of the lost-in-mourning Mrs Nelles—

NELLES: (*Sighing*) Wait outside, dear, and I'll check the
cupboard—

BOSCH: —the woman says, not stirring, never stirring,
as the starving mice chatter and patter about her—

NELLES: (*Noting package delivered*) Oh, is that the
cyanide I ordered, dear?

WICKER: (*Calling back through door*) It be, Mrs Nelles!
Problem with the mice?

NELLES: (*Darkly to self*) Oh the poison's not for them.

LEAP: Dear Lord, watch over our grieving Mrs Nelles,
whose loss has so consumed her. See that her black

thoughts, spiraling ever down toward self-destruction, are turned, once more, to the Light—

TOOM: *(To heavens)* —and while You're at it, Lord, get the old hen to open the public house—we'd kill our mothers for a drop!

BOSCH: *(In the public house)* Here drink once flowed but the doors have been shut tight ever since her daughter perished—

NELLES: *(To self)* Lavender, my dear...dead girl...

BOSCH: And now she sits alone, and sips her tea—

LEAP: —and the miserable town's kept miserably sober by the only one with a license to sell.

TOOM: Tis a crime is what it is.

NELLES: Call it what you will, but if you knew my love...you'd know my misery...

LEAP: *(With aching heart)* And if only you knew my love, my darling Mrs –*(Interrupting self)* Christ in heaven, is there even a difference between love and misery...

(WICKER coughs.)

NELLES: *(Who never got up from chair)* Still lurking outside, dear!?

WICKER: *(Dutifully)* I'm waiting for my biscuit.

NELLES: *(With edge)* There are no biscuits! Are you daft! Now scramoosh!

TRICITY: Vicar Leap! Oh Vicar, Hurry, it's Most Urgent!

(TRICITY enters.)

BOSCH: That must be the town's laundry maid, who every day at this time comes seeking assistance.

LEAP: What is it, Miss Tiara!

TRICITY: It's Armitage! He's trapped! Oh, you've got to help!

HOOTHER: *(Jauntily)* And clouds!—cumulus and cumulo-nimbus—shift shape as they float high...on the page...in a series of eight hundred plates by van Houten— Afternoon as defined by Ridley and Croon... has commenced!

(Lights up on LEAP, TOOM, *and* TRICITY *gathered at the door of the town privy.* ARMITAGE *is inside, banging on the door, while* TOOM *is working at the door with a crowbar.)*

ARMITAGE: *(From inside)* Help! Help!

LEAP: How is it possible, Mister Shanks, to get stuck in the Town Privy every week?!

ARMITAGE: Please for God's Sake, I can't breathe!

TOOM: Aye, no one can after you use the bog—

LEAP: Less chat, Mister Stoup.

TRICITY: Hang on dearest! *(To* LEAP*)* He's claustrophobic, you know.

LEAP: I know.

ARMITAGE: It's stuck fast! I've been trying for over an hour!

TOOM: *(Helpfully)* Try clenching your bottom, or wiggling from side to side—

ARMITAGE: I'm talking about the door!

TRICITY: Don't panic!

(And with a grunt, TOOM *at last flings open the door)*

ARMITAGE: Angel!

TRICITY: My darling!

*(*ARMITAGE *falls into* TRICITY's *arms. Whenever they are together, all is awfully dramatic—but it's crucial, of course, that they are always sincere, and as natural as possible, in*

their delivery. They're just young and innocent is what they are.)

ARMITAGE: Twas so dark!

TRICITY: But so much darker for me!

ARMITAGE: Love laughs at locksmiths!

TRICITY: As larks live by leeks, so lovers live by love! And now we're together!

ARMITAGE: Praise be thanks!

BOSCH: Witness the town lovers! — Miss Tricity Tiara, and Mister Armitage Shanks.

TRICITY: I never want to be apart again!

ARMITAGE: As Leander loved Hero, I'd swim through storming sea for you! Yet promise me—

TRICITY: Anything!

ARMITAGE: That we'll never yield to the conventions of the Age.

TRICITY: Perish the thought! —The Greatest Sin two Lovers can commit…

TRICITY/ARMITAGE: —is to marry!

BOSCH: Then how long will you stay together?

TRICITY: Til one of us finds another.

ARMITAGE: *(Great solemnity)* And if ever such a day should come—

TRICITY: *(Great solemnity)* We will part.

ARMITAGE: *(Bravely)* Without bitterness.

BOSCH: *(Hugely dubious)* Without bitterness?

TRICITY: *(Quite sure)* And without a single tear.

(TRICITY and ARMITAGE prepare to kiss, but are interrupted by WICKER.)

WICKER: I've come for the breeks of Jarl van Hoother.

TRICITY: *(Handing over a pair of trousers)* And here they are. Freshly washed.

ARMITAGE: *(Shoving* WICKER*)* Now bugger off.

HOOTHER: The sun sets, see Halliwell and Ricketts. The world in a word—

WICKER: *(As he puts books and trousers through the lighthouse mailslot)*

Here are the books. And here are the breeks.

HOOTHER: —"Glorious"! And done.

BOSCH: A day. Like any other…and every other.

(Lights out on all but BOSCH *and* WICKER, *who's looking worse-for-wear.)*

BOSCH: *(Chipperly)* So? What do you think of Brood?

WICKER: I hate it.

BOSCH: You're the one who wanted more story!

WICKER: *(Indignant)* Where's my moother? What kind of chapter is this?!

BOSCH: It's entitled "Wicker's Comeuppance." No Hetty, just misery.

WICKER: *(Tearfully)* But that sounds awful.

BOSCH: *(Cheerily)* So we'll just be done with this, and I'll be on my—

WICKER: No! You promised! You're not going til that blink stops!

BOSCH: But—you said you hate it here!

WICKER: *(Fiercely)* I hate it everywhere. *(Pause, then low—)* You're not going til that blink stops.

BOSCH: But— *(Glaring)* Fine!

*(*BOSCH *looks up toward the lighthouse light blinking high above him. Sizes it up. Then blows very hard. Then blows a*

*few more times. Pathetically. Then earnestly tries to knock it
out with a single gob of spit.* WICKER *looks on quizzically at*
BOSCH's *ineffectual efforts.* BOSCH *glares again at* WICKER,
*then heads determinedly to the lighthouse door. Tries it.
It's locked. Peers up at blinking light and* HOOTHER, *out of
patience.*)

BOSCH: (*Shouts to unhearing* HOOTHER) Think I'll let you
keep tending that ember!? (*Thinking*) How to snuff out
a blink. Urine? Nay. Stomping with boot? Nay. I'm
left with no choice but to accomplish it...narratively.
(*Thinking, to self*) I'm needing something merciless.
Something to flush him out so I can storm in, dash up,
and douse that ember once and for all!

WICKER: (*Triumphantly*) But he never opens his door!

BOSCH: (*Devising a plan*) What's been known to visit a
man unexpectedly, then worm its way through every
defense til it collars the heart? What spellbinding force
exists in Creation that can make a man do things he
wouldn't imagine doing in a million years?

WICKER: What?

BOSCH: A salesman. The title of the last chapter—
(*Pointing to lighthouse, triumphantly*) "Tis a Salesman
That'll Snuff It!"

WICKER: (*Hopefully*) You mean the title isn't "Wicker's
Comeuppance?"

BOSCH: That's the subtitle. (*Narrating with all his powers*)
Twas just betweesh the late and early when our
salesman first arrived in the town of Brood...the town
so quiet you could hear, clear across the way, the flap
of wings, from Mister Padgell's dream about a moth.
And yet...by first cock crow...not a nook or corner had
been spared the salesman's hand...

(Town revealed strewn with pamphlets. The villagers find them on the street, in their clothes, teapots, etc. Ominous music and sound effects increase as they read—)

TRICITY: "It is terrible, it is unthinkable, yet as more and more information/comes to light—

ARMITAGE: "—it is increasingly impossible to ignore—"

LEAP: "—Several coffins randomly unearthed in Durham—

NELLES: "In the Ipswich cemetery, a young boy—

ARMITAGE: "—scratchmarks on the inside of the lid—

TOOM: "—bloody nails—

TRICITY: "—found her face down—

NELLES: "—ominous knockings from below the ground—"

TOOM: "The Ipswich Nine—

ARMITAGE: "—the unmistakable signs—

LEAP: "….of premature burial."

NELLES: "Dear citizens, I've come to acquaint you with the most horrible death known to man."

TRICITY: "—the incontestable proof—"

LEAP: "—that good people throughout the land have been—

TOOM: "—buried alive…."

TRICITY: "The chartered company of Bodum and Wattney—"

NELLES: "—renowned makers of music boxes and clockwork automata—"

LEAP: "—have turned their considerable talents toward responding to this national emergency,"

ARMITAGE: "—and can announce that a remedy is at last at hand."

TOOM: "The Bodum and Wattney Patented Bell Device."

BOSCH: Yes, a salesman had arrived! A prophet of doom! A promiser of salvation! That's his game, now what's the name stenciled on his calling card!?

(Lights up on MISS SPOON, *with carpetbag, and the Bodum & Wattney strongbox under her arm)*

SPOON: *(Curtsying)* "Miss Anna Livia Spoon, licensed agent."

BOSCH: *(Panicked)* No! You're supposed to be a man! With a beard!

TOOM: *(Comparing photograph of Hetty he stole from* WICKER *with* SPOON*)* Leeze me on, don't she look familiar.

WICKER: *(So very excited)* My moother! I knew she'd show up!

BOSCH: *(Insistent)* Her name's Spoon. She's nothing to do with your mother.

WICKER: You'll see—that'll just be part of the twist is all!

*(*WICKER *runs off to follow* SPOON. *We see* TRICITY *gossiping to* ARMITAGE—*)*

TRICITY: She's taken up lodgings in the public house of Mrs Nelles.

ARMITAGE: But no one's boarded there for years.

(We see NELLES *speaking with* LEAP *in the public house)*

NELLES: That's what I told her, but then she took my hand and said—

SPOON: "I am asking you, for a moment…to trust me.…"

NELLES: And before I knew it, she had put her arms around me...held me close...

SPOON: (*Softly, with mysterious intensity*) "Believe me, my dear one...I understand...more than most...the devastation that comes...from a personal loss."

TRICITY: Reduced her to tears!

NELLES: She then said she had written out a few requirements regarding her room.

SPOON: "I shall be in by ten, when I shall expect from my room total darkness, total silence, total stillness, for I am...what is known as...a light sleeper..."

LEAP: And then what did you do?

NELLES: Well I took her bags upstairs of course.

SPOON: And my umbrella.

NELLES: She said she would need her appetite for dinner. Everything else I could take.

WICKER: (*Reciting to self*) The Bodum and Wattney Salesmanship Primer, Axiom Number One:

SPOON: "A foot in the door—half the battle has been won with that."

BOSCH: And the daintier the foot?

SPOON: The easier to slip it in.

BOSCH: And if they try to shut you out?

SPOON: Oh there's no shutting me out.

BOSCH: (*Suspicious*) You're sure the spitting image of Hetty alright...

SPOON: I hope you don't go spitting at me, Mister Tinker, (*Handing flyer to him*) I've only your interests at heart.

BOSCH: (*Handing flyer back—*) Yeah? And what about van Hoother's interests? Here's his door. He never opens it, so how are you gettin in?

SPOON: Oh I've a notion or two. It's getting to you that's the puzzler. (*Handing flyer again*) Will you not consider, sir, the possibility of one day being mistaken for dead?

BOSCH: (*Politely returning flyer*) Oh I mistake myself for dead all the time. Listen, little miss—Here's all I'm asking—as soon as you weasel into the lamphouse, give me a shout. You see, I've got some business with the bastard.

SPOON: Oh I'm sure you've got some business with us all. Every soul we meet shall play a part in our salvation.

BOSCH: Eh?

SPOON: Axiom Eight.

BOSCH: Do we have an arrangement or not?

LEAP: (*From afar*) Mister Stoup! Where in God's Name are you?!

(SPOON *winks, and exits*)

TOOM: (*Engrossed in booklet*) It's a blinking miracle!

(BOSCH *watches the next scene from nearby gravestone.* LEAP *makes his way to the graveyard, quite out of sorts, while* TOOM, *oblivious to* LEAP's *shouting, is thoroughly engrossed in his booklet—*)

LEAP: Didn't you hear me shouting?! I need to ask you if—Mister Stoup!

(*Eyes alight,* TOOM *holds up the catalogue in front of* LEAP's *face*)

LEAP: *(Reading)* "The Bodum and Wattney Winter Season Catalogue" *(Muttering)* —that woman will be the death of me.

TOOM: *(Excitedly)* Keep reading.

LEAP: *(Reading)* "Music Boxes, fine automata—

TOOM: *(Interrupting eagerly)* And you're wondering, "Just what is 'fine automata'?"

LEAP: I couldn't be less interested—

TOOM: Jaw-Dropping Mechanical Miracles, that's what. Look at this. Number Two-Seventeen.

LEAP: *(Reluctantly reads)* "Pig polishes boot."

(Beat)

TOOM: With brush.

LEAP: *(Reads, unenthusiastic)* "With brush."

TOOM: *(Snatching catalogue back and reads with fervor)* "Dressed in German fashion. Head turns, lifts boot for inspection. Spits. Polishes. Puts down boot."

LEAP: Yes.

TOOM: And it's a pig, you know.

LEAP: Yes.

TOOM: And then it starts all over again. The spit, the brush, all of it.

LEAP: Fine.

TOOM: And then after that? It does it again.

LEAP: Fine.

TOOM: And again after that.

LEAP: Fine.

TOOM: And bloody again after—

LEAP: *(Interrupting)* I know, I know, and it's a pig!—

TOOM: *(Eyes shining)* Aye, it's a pig. And it's real slaver comes out of it too.

LEAP: Splendid. But look, what I came here to ask you—

TOOM: And it's only fifteen groats.

LEAP: What's your point—surely you don't want one of these things—

TOOM: By "German Fashion" they mean Lederhosen.

LEAP: All of us starving to death, and the one thing you—

TOOM: Vicar, I've never been more serious in my whole holy life.

LEAP: *(Dumbfounded)* But you don't have a grey groat to your name—

TOOM: Don't you worry about the groats—I'll find a way.

LEAP: That's precisely what worries me— *(He stops short, for he suddenly notices—)* What in Heaven's name is that doing here.

TOOM: That? It's a bell device.

LEAP: I know it's a bell device. What's it doing here.

TOOM: Well not to oversimplify, but it sits on top of a grave, you see, and this bell connects to this wire that runs down this tube and into the coffin where it connects to a string, wrapped round the finger of the flodge who's down there having a moulder. Now if one sunny day the flodge wakes up and finds "hey ho, I'm not so dead after all," he can pull the string which triggers the bell which sends us all scampering up the hill with our spades to dig him up and buy him a drink.

LEAP: Mr. Stoup, I know. I mean what is it doing here.

TOOM: Tis a demonstration model. Miss Spoon brought it by and we set it up.

LEAP: Well I didn't give permission for that. I want it down by dusk.

TOOM: What? But Vicar, it aids in sales!

LEAP: Since when did we go into the bell device business! Now take it down.

TOOM: But what's the harm in a simple bell d—

LEAP: Oh sure! Yes! By all means! Let's drum up more panic and hysteria—that's just what I need! Good Lord, this morn alone I had six parishioners hounding me to exhume their loved ones and look for signs of premature burial!

TOOM: And can you blame them!

LEAP: The dead are dead!

TOOM: Except when they're not! Miss Spoon says gobs of things make you appear dead as a post, when in actuality—

LEAP: —when in actuality the dead don't know how good they've got it!

TOOM: (Whistles) That's quite a mood you're in, Vicar— didn't you get your breakfast this morning?

LEAP: Course I didn't get my breakfast, every cupboard in town is— (Suspicious—) Why, did you?

TOOM: I had a little something.

LEAP: Let me guess—Spoon had an extra kipper for anyone willing to put up a bell device.

TOOM: Ah, you make it sound like a bribe.

LEAP: What a miserable day. And to top it off, my History's missing.

TOOM: Your what?

LEAP: *(Impatiently)* My life's work. My History of Brood.

TOOM: That old thing? What about it.

LEAP: *(Out of patience)* It's missing! *(Desperate)* You haven't seen it, have you?

TOOM: *(Shrugging)* Where'd you see it last?

LEAP: On my desk! In the Vicarage! Where it always is!

TOOM: Now now, don't get excited. What about the little men?

LEAP: *(Gritted teeth)* I'm tired of telling you, there are no little men. And why would the little men take my book?!

TOOM: Well that's something you'll have to ask…the little men.

LEAP: I'm going to slit my wrists.

TOOM: *(Producing a flower from his pocket)* Ah cheer up, Vicar—look at this…Bluebells! Miss Spoon says she found a whole patch of 'em just bloomin away. Dontcha see? Spring! It's finally coming!

LEAP: *(Beginning to exit, muttering—)* We have no Spring. Sheep falling off cliffs and men falling off after them. We do have that.

TOOM: *(Calling out)* Oh Vicar, I was wondering—

LEAP: *(Sighing)* Yes, Mister Stoup.

TOOM: Did I tell you the poor box is missing?

LEAP: No.

TOOM: Well…the poor box is missing.

BOSCH: *(Brooding)* Bluebells…we were up to our ears in bluebells weren't we, Hetty—that picnic on the bluff, when I lofted that daftest of questions: "Will you Marry me." If only I could crack the mystery

of your answer. I trample you with horses, maroon
you on islands, send you into the arms of a hundred
blackguards, it doesn't make a difference—every
morning you're coming back to me tonight, and every
night you're coming back to me in the morning and
every day the same...old...excrement. "Will you marry
me." The wonder and terror of the universe sweeping
over me as I clutched the stems of those bluebells and
awaited your answer—

(SPOON *stifles a laugh through her nose. Any spell of
sentimentality is broken.*)

BOSCH: *(Angrily)* Got something in your nose?!

SPOON: *(Bemused)* Oh I've nothing but respect for your
poetical temperament. *(Handing flyer)* Indeed, you're
just the fellow for a Bodum and Wattney automata.

BOSCH: My memories are just a big pig polishing a
boot, is that it.

SPOON: I'm sure I didn't mean to suggest that.

BOSCH: *(Flinging back flyer)* Stay out of it. It's Hoother's
door you should be hammering. *(Dander up)* And yes, I
do like winding up me little memories. Watching Hetty
say, for instance—

SPOON: *(Guessing)* "I love you Tom, and always have.
Of course I'll marry you."

BOSCH: Or watching her as she turns around and
gives us a wink, that last time, before disappearing...
for a "brief but unavoidable errand." "A brief but
unavoidable errand."...

(SPOON *exits discreetly.* BOSCH *broods/puzzles out—*)

BOSCH: Disappearing... Without a trace...not weeks
after a wregling struggled out of her, red as a cherry
and bawling his eyes out-

(WICKER *approaches, bawling. His hand is stuck in the poor box. It will remain stuck until the last pages of the play.*)

WICKER: *(Weeping)* Mister Bosch! The poorbox from the kirk—

BOSCH: *(Hardly caring)* I see you've got your hand stuck in it.

WICKER: I do have my hand stuck in it!

BOSCH: Well you'll be catching it hard from the Vicar—

WICKER: I need a Boodum and Watney! I doon't want to be alive when I die!

BOSCH: So you've met our Miss Spoon, have you.

WICKER: *(Mood changes immediately)* She's loovely! I thought you said it was going to be a man. But she's not a man.

BOSCH: No, she's not a man.

WICKER: I thought you said it was going to be a man.

BOSCH: Well I was wrong! I thought you were going to be a man instead of a sack of wet undergarments, but there you go.

WICKER: I don't knoo why you're so mean all the time. I don't knoo what I did—

BOSCH: Well for starters, you got *born*! You got born the son of a shank of a sailor—

WICKER: He wasn't a shank!

BOSCH: He married the lousy woman I was going to marry, then scramooshed before you were hardly a bump—

WICKER: It's not my fault!

BOSCH: Oh, and keeping me in this lousy tale isn't your fault either I suppose!

WICKER: *(Brightening)* Oh but it's just getting good! Now that moother is here—

BOSCH: She's not your mother.

WICKER: Oh but she is! She hugs me, and that's how my mum really looked, isn't it! And how she talked?

BOSCH: No.

WICKER: And how she stood—

BOSCH: No.

WICKER: And her smile—

BOSCH: Quiet! No! …yes…fine…I can hardly look at her… But I'm telling you, she's not your mother.

WICKER: But there was that chapter when moother got kicked in the bonce by the donkey and she forgot who she was—remember? And that other time, when the tree fell on her bonce and she forgot who she was—remember? That's what this is.

BOSCH: Aye. Except it isn't. Hey, did she tell you her scheme for Hoother?

WICKER: *(Shaking head)* She was picking a flower.

BOSCH: A flower?

WICKER: A bluebell.

BOSCH: Christ she's good. *(Thinking)* Let me guess… you then went straight away to Jarl van's to deliver his books.

(Lights up on HOOTHER, *studying his books in the lighthouse)*

HOOTHER: A new Ferguson and Ives!— "Illustrations and Classifications to supplement the ever-growing Inventory of Natural Things. In this appendix—"Moths and How they Flap. Diagrams On the Exquisite Design of the Donkey, Toothed Snails, Hairy Snails"…"—

(HOOTHER *turns the page and is stunned. Holds up a letter he has found between pages*)

BOSCH: You see what she's done—he wouldn't take anything but his Fergusons up the stairs, so she slipped it 'tween the pages...

HOOTHER: *(Reads letter, agape—)* "...My dear...Mister... van Hoother..."

(HOOTHER *now notices a bluebell enclosed with letter. He holds it up, stares intensely.*)

BOSCH: *(Relishing)* Oh aye...that bluebell will pull the bung from his boat...

WICKER: *(Half to self)* If he's never been outside, he's never seen a flower....

BOSCH: *(Watching Hoother's reaction)* He's seen a million flowers in those books of his, and their Latin name besides.

WICKER: I mean a real one.

BOSCH: *(Relishing)* No, never a real one. He's never seen a real anything...

(And as HOOTHER *continues to stare at the bluebell—)*

WICKER: Axiom 74, as related by Miss Spoon—

SPOON: "Make sure to leave a little something behind. Gifts play miraculously on the mind."

(HOOTHER, *staring at bluebell, is in mortal terror— breathing and swallowing heavily*)

HOOTHER: ...what's the matter, Jarl van.... *(Swallows)* ...it's just a campinula rotundifolia.... The only difference between this one and the one in volume 78... is that this one isn't labeled...

(His attempts to remain calm and rational turn into a torrent of words—for as he stares at flower [and he stares at flower exclusively through monologue)]he sees for the

*first time, with blinding force, the bewildering immensity
and cold ambivalence of the universe. We hear, building
underneath—humming hive, bird shriek, lightning crack,
whinny of dying animal, roar of burning stars, etc—sounds
that connote terrorful, buzzing existence)*

HOOTHER: We'll review…The World in a Word.
"Sensible." *(Referring to bluebell)* We have a flower—
we'll break it down. *(Reminding self)* Sensible. *(Quickly)*
Just begin with the stem, no no, begin with the seed
that leads to the stem, No, begin with the pollen that
leads to the seed, or no, begin with the bee, yes! with
pollinating bombinating bee, chancing upon a sea of
bluebells and returning to the hive, yes!, begin with
the hive, and the hum of the hive, alive, the frantic
buzzing and within, the larval writhing of eyeless—no!
begin with the roots of the bluebell, yes, the water,
the rain, the roiling clouds, yes begin with lightning
crack, the undiscriminating fury, yes, begin with Fear,
no! begin with the leaves, yes, that capture light, yes,
begin with the sun, quite nice, quite yellow, quite vast
and blazing and terrorful, and around it hurtling the
dot of a planet and the spin of the planet begetting the
black of the night begetting the sight of the damning
immensity of space and stars and no stay focused! the
World in a Word… *(Softly)* "chaos". No! No. *(Newly
determined)* Begin with the stem, the two fingers that
uproot the stem, to insert in a book, yes, begin with
the fingers, the skin, the flesh, the woman—yes begin
with Miss Spoon, yes begin with chills, trembling,
nausea— No! *(The sound effects cut out)* End with Miss
Spoon. *(Quickly setting pen to paper)* "Dear Miss Spoon,
thank you for your letter, do not send any more.
Yours, Jarl van Hoother." *(Begins to fold letter, unfolds
it, and writes threateningly—)* "P S: I shall warn you
only once, madam!" —no. *(He crosses it out)* "P S: I've
changed my mind, please continue with your letters.

With specimens." *(Begins to fold letter, unfolds it, writes quickly—)* "Despite", underscore, "My Emphatic Wish that You do Not." *(Pause)* Good. *(Correcting—)* And not "yours", but "yours respectfully", no, "yours— ", *(Then occurring—)* No! Not yours! Not yours at all! Not yours at all! *(He crumples up the paper violently, and tosses it on desk. Stares at it. Moves it to further part of desk. Stares at it. Finally, stands, picks paper up, contemplates it, then shoves it in his trousers pocket, wipes his hands of the whole affair.)*

BOSCH: So that's your plan.

SPOON: You have to introduce them to a little life before they can start dreading their death.

BOSCH: *(Pleased)* Look at him quake—he's your quarry now—

SPOON: "Quarry" indeed—I'm here to save lives. And not just his. The entire village beckons!

LEAP: Yet after a day of door-to-door—

SPOON: —did I manage to sell a bell and make my quota? I did not.

LEAP: And to what did she attribute this?

SPOON: Poverty and pig-headedness.

TOOM: And after bamfing through bogs and over hillocks, could she sleep this first night?

NELLES: She could not.

SPOON: Not a wink.

TRICITY: And to what did she attribute this?

SPOON: The blink of the lighthouse blinking into the room.

BOSCH: I don't like it—I need you at the top of your game!

SPOON: I can't explain it—the shades were down and I was wearing my nightmask.

BOSCH: *(Suddenly suspicious)* And was there another who couldn't sleep, who spent all the night aneath the window of Miss Spoon?

(Lights up on ARMITAGE *by* SPOON's *window, caught by surprise)*

ARMITAGE: *(Gasps)* I was just strolling by!

BOSCH: Were you now.

ARMITAGE: *(Confiding)* She makes a point, you have to admit. I can't sleep thinking about it.

BOSCH: About dying prematurely?

ARMITAGE: About the touch of her hand, when she told me to trust her…

BOSCH: And Grigs? How's the night for you?

*(*WICKER *still has poorbox stuck on hand)*

WICKER: It's blashy out, and I'm cold.

BOSCH: *(Hopefully)* So you want to stop all this blether then?

WICKER: *(Newly resolute)* Nay!

BOSCH: Stubborn calf!

(At BOSCH's *subtle cue,* TOOM *seizes* WICKER *and hauls him away)*

TOOM: You're in for it now, bishop!

BOSCH: *(Threateningly)* On to Day Two!

(Lights up on NELLES *and* LEAP *in public house, sipping from tea cups. Porcelain figurines are on the table.)*

NELLES: *(Steeping in memories)* Lavender did so love these figurines of hers….

LEAP: *(Unable to see why)* Well it's easy to see why. They're very......well it's wonderful craftsmanship, isn't it.

NELLES: All porcelain.

LEAP: And they're playing some sort of quartet, I gather.

NELLES: Yes, and that one's got a baton and little nose-specks.

LEAP: Yes.

(Beat)

NELLES: And they're pigs, you know.

LEAP: *(Politely)* Yes, yes I noticed.

(Pause)

NELLES: ...it was such a little cough...I mean, I worried. She was such a wisp of a thing...dreamy, you know...

LEAP: I never saw her without a book...

NELLES: But I didn't think it would...

(NELLES trails off, grieving)

LEAP: *(Consoling)* There was nothing you could do—

NELLES: I'm quite sure there was.

LEAP: And twas a long time ago besides.

NELLES: Oh I wouldn't say that.

LEAP: *(Gently)* I know you wouldn't, but everyone else would. Trust me...it's been a long time. *(Consolingly)* Lavender's in Heaven now...with a library of books and all the pig figurines she could ever—

NELLES: I want her dug up.

LEAP: Oh God not you too—

NELLES: *(Pleading)* We buried her alive—I need to see her, Enry—

LEAP: No one's getting dug up in this town—

NELLES: I can't rest....I think of her scratching away in the dark...crying out for her mum—

LEAP: Doctor O'Connell pronounced your daughter dead! It was consumption. Lavender died. The good doctor, god rest his soul, was unerring.

NELLES: Aye, bless his heart, and surely we could do with a doctor in this town now. But Doctor O'Connel was also a five foot five inch walking bottle of alcohol. He couldn't make it down a road at night without molesting a tree.

LEAP: Well... *(Conceding)* Aye... But he knew what dead looked like.

NELLES: He knew what the bottom of a glass looked like. Back when this public house was open, he was always the first to arrive and the last to leave—

LEAP: *(Overcome)* Hoo...that's right...this very room was humming with people, wasn't it...Oh, those were times, weren't they Mrs Nelles. Great larks we—

NELLES: I despised every moment.

LEAP: That's not how it looked to us. You presided over it all like an apron-clad queen!

NELLES: *(Modestly)* Oh I don't know about that.

LEAP: *(Angling)* I mean deep down, you must miss it— the glowing faces, the music—

NELLES: Well, aye, there was laughter—

LEAP: *(Encouraged)* —laughter galore. And all the gang with their sonnets and blousting—

NELLES: Jigs on the table—

LEAP: Jovial shoving —

NELLES: *(Coming to senses)* —you mean fistfights—

LEAP: *(Still in reverie)* Flying crockery—

NELLES: Broken crockery, and great pools of up-throw I was left to clean up. Nightly.

LEAP: *(By-the-by)* So do you think you'll be re-opening any time soon?

NELLES: Enry, a thousand times, No.

LEAP: *(Backtracking)* T'isn't that I don't appreciate a cup of tea as much as the next man, but...wait a minute... that's not...you're not drinking tea at all, are you...

NELLES: Of course I am.

LEAP: No you're not. That's... *(Agape)* ...that's whiskey! *(Outraged)* You old bird!—

NELLES: *(Shrugging simply)* I prefer the taste of it.

LEAP: *(Forgetting all decorum)* "I prefer the—?! Is that all you have to say for yourself?! *(Gasps as full significance hits him)* You've been quietly sipping through your entire stock!

NELLES: *(Sly grin)* Oh very quietly.

LEAP: But meanwhile Brood's been as dry as an empty bucket!

NELLES: I'm not discussing that!

LEAP: Well *I'm* discussing it!

NELLES: *I'm* discussing my murdered daughter!

LEAP: *(Out of patience)* I'm telling you, she was already dead!

NELLES: If you won't grant me my simple request!—

LEAP: —to gawk at some ooze that was once your daughter?! Aye, the answer's no!

NELLES: Then I want you out.

LEAP: What? Mrs Nelles—

NELLES: Out. Yes—right now. Christ in Heaven, are the bottles all anyone cares about!?

LEAP: All I care about is the unmitigated Glory that is You! Marry me, for god's sake, marry me and these peltry skies will be nothing but sun for the rest of our days! *(Now more evidently to self)* That's what I'd say if I had one vertebrae to call my own. *(Appalled)* "She's in Heaven now with all the pig figurines—"—jesus god Leap can you be a bigger prat. Oh Fanny, I could swim in your eyes til Thursday…but instead I'll just stammer out an apology *(Standing and gathering his things)* and disguise every one of my feelings with some insipid gossip like— *(To* NELLES*)* "Oh and by the way—Miss Tiara says she saw your boarder Miss Spoon today… She was wading up to her thighs in tidepools."

BOSCH: *(Lightbulb flash)* "Tidepools"?!

LEAP: Now is that a woman to put your confidence in? "I'm catching sea snails," she said.

BOSCH: *(To* SPOON*)* Out with it, woman! You're Hetty Grigs!

SPOON: Who?

BOSCH: *(Waggling finger)* No no, none of that. You had me going for a bit, but Wicker was right. Look at you, with those skirts hitched up—looking just like you did that time we romped about in the pools. Remember that one, Hetty?

SPOON: Em….no.

BOSCH: One, ONE Chapter without you would've been nice, but you've got to go and prance in front of me every single time.

SPOON: What's the harm in collecting snails?

BOSCH: So this is the plot for this one, is it, Het?

SPOON: I believe you're mistaking me for someone else.

BOSCH: Interesting. Denying your identity, posing as "Spoon, the Pretty Pedlar"? What happened?

SPOON: Nothing happened!

BOSCH: Were you hit on the bonce? Or are you trying to forge a new life, as far away from your bairn and betrothed as you can?

SPOON: I have to go.

BOSCH: Confound it! You said you'd be back before my little tinker's fire died out! Well I've been throwing fuel on my little fire and making up bloody adventures for you ever since! So what was it! Marauding Pirates?! Highwaymen!? A carnivorous haddock?!—that was chapter ninety-eight—that was a good one—

SPOON: You poor thing—you're addled. *(A little secret)* You know, if you could open my box, you'd be done with these questions.

BOSCH: *(Amused)* Your box? What kind of smut are you talking now? Come on, woman, it's answers I'm wanting!

(Lights up on TRICITY *washing clothes by the stream)*

TRICITY: *(Picking up stockings)* "I am the hose of Vicar Leap...in need of a darning." And you? "I am the camisole of the celebrated Miss Spoon." "Oh of course Miss Spoon, t'would be an honor to wash your underthings. *(Taking out a little scissors and cutting through camisole)* ...Though pity about the rip down the back—accidents do happen." *(Now picking up pants)* And you, I'd know you anywhere. The mysterious trousers of the mysterious Jarl van, now there's a man... A man who's never met another, imagine that. *(More introspective)* A man who'll never need another... imagine that... *(Changing tone)* a man who never turns out his pockets before sending them on... *(Finding crumpled piece of paper)* oh, and what do we have today?

Funny notes about the squirrelfish? *(She reads—)* "Dear
Miss Spoon…" *(To self, as she scans letter)* Of all the…
(To heavens) What is this town coming to?!

*(ARMITAGE enters bounding, dressed in painter's smock,
carrying an easel and half-finished portrait.)*

ARMITAGE: My Thisbe, my Daphne, my Dearest Duck!

TRICITY: Armitage, what is it about her that every man
in Brood finds so appealing!?

*(ARMITAGE sets up easel and TRICITY assumes pose they've
clearly already practiced—)*

ARMITAGE: *(Painting)* Miss Spoon? I wouldn't know.

TRICITY: Really. She could blow a kiss to the sea and
you'd all dive in after it.

ARMITAGE: She *can* be rather persuasive.

TRICITY: *(Alarmed)* You're not still thinking of buying—

ARMITAGE: —a bell device, I am. Don't move, my pet.

TRICITY: But the cost—

ARMITAGE: I have my inheritance—

TRICITY: Yes, and a responsibility not to throw it away
on trifles!

ARMITAGE: Tis no trifle to die in a box! But perhaps it's
only my money you care about—

TRICITY: *(Bursting into tears)* Oh how could you say
such a thing!

ARMITAGE: *(Near tears himself)* No no, don't cry my
darling! I didn't mean it!

TRICITY: *(Shattered)* If that's what you think, then better
we parted ways!—buy a bell, I don't care…

ARMITAGE: *(Shaken to core, the world is over)* Oh I've said
something thoughtless and now I've dashed our love
to pieces!

TRICITY: *(Desperate, weeping wildly)* No darling, don't believe it!

ARMITAGE: *(Utterly disconsolate, tears raining down)* And now I don't care if I die in a box because what's life without life with you!

TRICITY: *(Tears)* Oh Armitage, do you mean it?

ARMITAGE: *(Tears)* With all my heart.

TRICITY: *(Drying tears)* Then maybe instead of buying a bell, *(Completely recovered)* …we should get a boat.

ARMITAGE: A what?

TRICITY: We could pack it with all sorts of nice things and have a row down the stream—

ARMITAGE: An outing!

TRICITY: It's been so long—We could have a picnic on Ruesdael's Bluff—

ARMITAGE: And gaze up at the clouds—

TRICITY: Or each other's eyes—

ARMITAGE: Til the sun descends…

TRICITY: How does that sound?

ARMITAGE: Like heaven! Still, tis no trifle to die in a box.

TRICITY: I would never let you die in a box.

ARMITAGE: Nor I, you. Like Orpheus, I'd travel to the underworld itself to rescue you!

TRICITY: Then you promise you won't think of seeing that mucky old Spoon again?

ARMITAGE: Fine. Yes. I'll tell her tonight.

TRICITY: What?

ARMITAGE: Straight off.

TRICITY: What do you mean you'll tell her tonight?

ARMITAGE: When she comes. That she needn't come again.

TRICITY: But she needn't come at all!

ARMITAGE: But we already made plans. Twould be rude to beg out of them now.

TRICITY: I wish you wouldn't.

ARMITAGE: Oh but why my peach? Don't you trust me?

TRICITY: I don't trust her. She'll use every spell in her book to get you to commit. Please, promise me you won't meet with her.

ARMITAGE: But… Oh all right, I promise.

TRICITY: Good. Mind you, I don't want to stand in your way. If it's that you fancy her—

ARMITAGE: But I don't care a fig for her!

TRICITY: *(Relieved)* O Armitage— Honestly?

ARMITAGE: *(Seductively)* I don't know what you might have seen or heard, but just as Procris…daughter of Artemis…thought she overheard Cephalus make cooing phrases to a maiden when in fact it was only a breeze, so I say to you…twas only a breeze…

TRICITY: Kiss me.

(ARMITAGE *flings down his brushes, but before he and* TRICTY *can kiss* WICKER *enters still with poorbox*)

WICKER: I've come for the breeks of Jarl van Hoother.

TRICITY: They're not ready yet.

ARMITAGE: Now feck off.

(*A great rumble of thunder, we hear rain pouring down,* ARMITAGE *and* TRICITY *hurry off.*)

BOSCH: And the rain laughs down on this humorless town, as night descends.

WICKER: *(To* SPOON*)* And sure your name's not Hetty Grigs, Miss? Were you not maybe hit on the bonce?

SPOON: I'll hit you on the bonce if you keep asking me that. *(Now turning sympathetic)* Here… *(A little magic and she produces a withered carrot, which she hands to him)* …Have a carrot, little toad.

WICKER: Ooo thank you! I'll eat it tonight! And meanwhile I'll put it down me breeks for safekeeping!

*(*BOSCH *has grabbed a bottle [from the publichouse?], and has begun to drink)*

BOSCH: *(Narrating)* And an urchin spends the rest of the night looking for a carrot he put down his trousers for safekeeping. *(Holding in his own hand)* This carrot in fact. *(Calling out to frantically trouser-inspecting* GRIGS*)* Keep looking Grigs! There's a magic pocket in there somewhere! …Now tell me, woman, you found some sleep this third night in Brood, didn't you?

SPOON: Not a tick.

BOSCH: Well you weren't alone. For thanks to you—

(We hear distant moans and screams—"Let me out!" etc., growing louder and more frantic)

BOSCH: —the rest of the town rested restlessly—beset by nightmares of coffins and cramped confinements…

(Screams peak and abruptly end, lights up on HOOTHER.*)*

BOSCH: All except Jarl van Hoother, that bastard, still secure in his tower. A formidable foe, a man who never eats, never sleeps, who lives on tea—

HOOTHER: Good tea, this.

BOSCH: —a lone tea ball, that he steeps and steeps—

SPOON: *(Intrigued)* And he never sees a sliver of sleep?

BOSCH: Nay—always at the desk, at dawn and dusk, straining his brain to fit together every twitch, every flap of feather in this Wide Winking World—

HOOTHER: *(Studying)* —from nothing, to egg, to grub, to bluebottle fly, see page four hundred five— *(He turns page and finds a letter from* SPOON, *and a small shell. Reads—)* "Dear Mister van Hoother—

HOOTHER/SPOON: "This is the third letter I've sent.

SPOON: *(As voice of letter)* I've yet to receive a reply. Still, I'm hopeful you will grant me an audience. Today I enclose a sea snail. I don't know its Latin name, although I'm sure you could enlighten me. I was told it's a dead language, Latin. Rather appropriate since this snail is dead. At least I believe so, having not seen it poke its head out. And for that matter, having not heard from you, I do hope you are not dead. Or are you simply hiding from danger? Lovely shell, don't you think? I enclose it for you—"

HOOTHER: *(Reading end of letter)* "—a keepsake to keep in your keep…Miss Spoon."

WICKER: *(Treating* HOOTHER's *"Miss Spoon" as first part of his sentence)* —doesn't sleep.

ARMITAGE: Miss Spoon—

NELLES: —doesn't eat.

TOOM: She's consumed with a quota—

LEAP: —she's yet to reach.

NELLES: Her fourth—

TOOM: —and fifth nights

BOSCH: How were they spent?

NELLES: I sang her lullabies.

SPOON: Don't ask how it went.

BOSCH: *(Concerned)* Still couldn't sleep?

SPOON: No.

NELLES: *(Indignant)* Blamed my lullabies.

SPOON: Also—

TOOM: Her lack of a sale.

LEAP: Sixty-one doors knocked—

NELLES: —to no avail.

ARMITAGE: And most of all—

NELLES: —she blamed—

SPOON: The horrible the beautiful blink of that lighthouse.

(Lights out. Then up briefly again, simulating a lighthouse blink. Out again. Up again on a tableau of LEAP in graveyard. Out again. Up again on LEAP in graveyard and, nearby, NELLES sneaking toward the graveyard, carrying a shovel, not noticing LEAP. Out again. Up again on NELLES surprised by LEAP, who is right beside her and just as surprised.)

LEAP: Mrs Nelles!? But you haven't been out of your house for years!

NELLES: *(Feigning innocence)* Oh?

LEAP: Fancy meeting you here. *(Gradually realizing)* In the graveyard. At mirk-night. With a shovel…

NELLES: Oh it's not really a shovel, it's more a walking stick really.

(Beat)

LEAP: *(Seizing shovel)* Give me that!

NELLES: I don't think so!

(As they struggle for the shovel with surprising force, winding up wrestling on the ground—)

LEAP: I'm not about to wrestle a lady, much less one in mourning!

NELLES: That's fine, cause baisting a man of the cloth makes me uneasy—

LEAP: Then what are you doing!

NELLES: I'm biding my time til you let go! What are you doing!

LEAP: I'm getting slathered in mud trying to help a woman come to her senses!

(Still wrestling as—)

NELLES: She never left the house! It was an inside consumption, and they're never fatal!

LEAP: "Inside consumption"? What kind of blether is that?! And Lavender must have gotten out from time to time…I mean, she wore an engagement ring—

(The wrestling has diminished.)

NELLES: Well that's Lavender for you isn't it.

LEAP: She had the whole town wondering who'd want to marry her—

NELLES: —which I'm sure delighted her no end… *(More introspective)* I don't know—maybe she was engaged but… *(Beat)* I guess we'll never know now… *(Reprovingly)* Silly girl…

(NELLES, still with grip on shovel, begins to cry. BOSCH is there, with bottle.)

LEAP: *(Gently)* Fanny… We die. Contrary to the claims of our salesman, we die.…

NELLES: I just need to see—

LEAP: Yes, because, against all reason, you think you might find a little pulse…a bit of breath… *(Gently)* But it's not going to happen… Now give me the shovel…

(Beat)

NELLES: Not on your bloody life!

LEAP: You confounded old crow!

(They wrestle with grunts of exertion, intensity and what seems like increasing…intimacy?…until, suddenly, LEAP kisses her, passionately. NELLES briefly requites just as ardently, until she pushes away)

NELLES: What do you think you're doing?!

LEAP: *(Aghast)* My mouth slipped! Twas a mistake!

NELLES: *(Suddenly not outraged, just curious)* Are you sure twas just a mistake?

LEAP: *(Picking up unexpected tone, confused—)* What do you mean, "am I sure?"

NELLES: *(Hearing something)* Ssh.

(In the distance, out of sight—)

ARMITAGE: *(Offstage)* Aaah! It just crawled under my shirt!

SPOON: *(Offstage)* Don't panic. Hoo! Look at those wings…

(LEAP and NELLES are peering toward offstage.)

LEAP: *(Bewildered, whispering)* Is that Mister Shanks?

NELLES: *(Whispering)* I believe so.

BOSCH: *(Peering toward offstage)* That's certainly our salesman—

LEAP: What in heaven's name is she doing out in the middle of—

NELLES: She has my cyanide, that's what.

LEAP: Your what?

NELLES: My lovely potassium cyanide. I had a whole tin of it. For the mice, you know.

LEAP: Mice indeed.

NELLES: But she kept pestering me cause she wanted it for her killing jar.

LEAP: Her what?

NELLES: Killing jar—to collect bugs and whatnot.

LEAP: Why in heaven's name would she want to collect bugs?

(Lights up on Hoother, penning a letter, with specimens nearby)

HOOTHER: Dear Miss Spoon, thank you for your luna moth, your tiger beetle, your birch weevil and leave me alone!

BOSCH: *(Nodding approvingly)* P S.

HOOTHER: Send…more…letters.

(HOOTHER looks at letter, then crumples it up. Thinks better, smoothes it out . Then crumples it again. WICKER, still with poorbox stuck on his hand, enters. BOSCH will be hitting the bottle for the rest of the act.)

WICKER: Mister Bosch.

BOSCH: What.

WICKER: I want my hand cut off.

BOSCH: *(Giving serious consideration)* A one-handed postal bairn? I don't think so.

WICKER: But I want this box off. I can't stand it anymore.

BOSCH: So go to the Vicar.

WICKER: He couldn't find the key to open it. And then he said he'd give me a baisting for stealing the box.

BOSCH: *(Not caring)* Aye, that's a shame.

WICKER: And then he couldn't find his stick, so he couldn't give me a baisting.

BOSCH: Well happy day!

WICKER: But then Toom said he could give me a baisting without a stick. And he did.

BOSCH: Well you're the one who insists on keeping this going—

WICKER: Cause if we stop, you're gone! I want the rest of the story—just somewhere else!

BOSCH: So take that road there out of town.

WICKER: Every road just lands me back here!

BOSCH: *(Maliciously)* And Welcome to Brood.

WICKER: Why are you doing this to me?!

BOSCH: You're doing it to me! *(Consoling self)* But Hoother can't last much longer—she sends him specimen after specimen, and he wants her to stop, but he doesn't want her to stop.

WICKER: Why?

BOSCH: Cause it's been proven the only reason we have brains…is so we can drive ourselves mad. And your mum—oh aye—your mum's an expert on brains.

(Lights up on HOOTHER, *who is finishing a book, his clean trousers folded nearby.)*

HOOTHER: Done. Make sure of it—done? *(Little disappointed)* Done… No letter? *(His laundered trousers catch his eye. He holds them up, and finds the pocket to be glowing. He pulls out a letter and vial containing glowing object. Reads—)* "Mr van Hoother—

SPOON: *(As voice of letter)* —this is the seventh letter I've been compelled to send since you seem incapable of the courtesy of a reply. Thoughts of you blink in my head throughout the day, and, worse, you nightly disturb my sleep with your light, so I've enclosed a little illumination of my own. A, hopefully, living specimen—"

HOOTHER: *(Intensely to self as he stares at vial)* ...lampyris noctiluca...

SPOON: "—one glowworm. They say the light allows the male to find his mate...I enclose this light for you....my sweet...my bewildering...my dismantling one....Miss Spoon..."

HOOTHER: *(Setting pen to paper)* Dear...Miss Spoon... Stay out of my trousers— *(Suddenly, a knocking on his door down below.)* What's that?...couldn't be.... She wouldn't be!... *(More knocking until finally—)* Right! *(He leaps from his desk. He hurries down thirty flights of stairs as—)* Never in all my days, Miss Spoon, do you hear?! This is beyond disregard, beyond disrespect, this is nothing less than a desecration of my most precious possession—my concentration! Your reckless usurpation of my books for private ends, your unforgivable trespass into my trousers and now this unprecedented display of door assault are ample confirmation that you are a creature never to be dealt with! Do I make myself clear?!

TRICITY: Perfectly. But I'm not Miss Spoon.

(Lights up on TRICITY at lighthouse door. The entire conversation below is conducted through the closed door of the lighthouse, and probably more effective if HOOTHER is hidden from audience's view.)

HOOTHER: What.

TRICITY: May I come in?

HOOTHER: *(Panicked)* No.

TRICITY: My name is Miss Tiara, and I've come for the backpay you owe me.

HOOTHER: How could I possibly owe you anything! All I ask is to be left alone!

TRICITY: That isn't true. You also ask that your trousers be laundered, so I've laundered them, foolishly respecting your privacy like everyone else— *(Brandishing his crumpled letter)* But having discovered you're actually encouraging correspondence, and from a salesman no less, I see no reason to be cowed by your reputation, and demand at last some sort of recompense.

(Pause)

HOOTHER: *(Agape at a world he had never considered)* You launder my trousers?

TRICITY: Did you think they laundered themselves?

(Pause)

HOOTHER: I hadn't really thought about it.

TRICITY: Yes, most boys are like that.

HOOTHER: *(Dander up)* Well I have this to say about your laundering service, madam! My trousers always come back… *(Pause, Now at a loss—)* …crisp and clean. *(Beat)* It's nice.

TRICITY: *(Still annoyed)* Thank you. It's called soap. Now, I've written out the amount you owe, and don't pretend you haven't got it—everyone knows you're sitting on a big bag of guilders.

HOOTHER: I have no guilders.

TRICITY: That's rubbish. How do you buy oil for your beacon.

HOOTHER: I don't. *(Confidentially)* That flame's burning on less than a teaspoon. I could blow it out with a breath, it's that delicate.

TRICITY: "The lonely guardian of a delicate flame" —that's very romantic you know.

HOOTHER: It's what?

TRICITY: Though you must be a bundle of nerves—tis a great responsibility.

HOOTHER: *(Shrugging)* I don't really think about it.

TRICITY: You don't think about much, do you.

HOOTHER: *(Dander up)* I don't think about—?! Do you have any idea what I'm doing up there?!

TRICITY: No.

HOOTHER: I'm fitting the world together!

TRICITY: How awfully clever of you. And are you close?

HOOTHER: Rather so. Or rather…no. *(Confidence collapsing)* In fact I'm beginning to wonder if I've been dead wrong about all of this. *(Pained)* Of late I've been feeling really awful.

TRICITY: You poor thing—what are your symptoms?

HOOTHER: *(Quickly)* Dizziness, trembling, sweating, choking, nausea, chills, chest pain—

TRICITY: Goodness! When did all this start?

HOOTHER: The same day I was sent a flower by post.

TRICITY: Perhaps it's an allergy.

HOOTHER: *(Hopefully)* To a flower?

TRICITY: *(Pointedly)* Or to the woman who sent you the flower.

HOOTHER: *(Despairing, panicked, yet relieved to confess it)* I can't concentrate! I look in my books at a lungfish or a sparrow, and suddenly they're not lungfishes and sparrows at all! Ten million species are just ten million disguises worn by one and the same thing…. Her!

TRICITY: But you don't even know what she looks like!

HOOTHER: Exactly! So I don't see her so much as feel her. She's behind it all! Unblinking, Unheeding, Unrelenting—or is that Life?

BOSCH: It's Death.

TRICITY: It's Love.

HOOTHER: What? *(Referring in head)* Wait—folio 8, volume 8, page 192....Snails.

TRICITY: Sorry?

HOOTHER: Snails. They're described as shooting "telum amoris" into each other. "Love darts." From the diagram, it appears excruciating—

TRICITY: But that sounds just like Cupid! Anyone hit by his arrow goes sick with love—

HOOTHER: So Love is some sort of parasite, like the larva of the Bott's Fly, am I right? Entering the bloodstream, then traveling to the brain?

TRICITY: Well...a little.

HOOTHER: So how do you get rid of it?!

BOSCH: Aye, how do you get rid of it!

TRICITY: But...but why would you want to?

HOOTHER: *(Exasperated)* Why?! Because it's intolerable!

(Lights up on ARMITAGE, preferably in privy, secretly penning a letter)

ARMITAGE: " ...my dear Miss Spoon... Twould be best if we meet away from the public glare, where we may, at last, discuss all that is in our hearts. There is a boat that I shall captain alone downstream with picnic hamper...By noon, I shall reach the Fingle Bridge, and if you await on the banks by that goodly bridge, we may proceed together undetected from there. Until tomorrow, I am, in sweet anticipation—

BOSCH: Hetty or Anna Livia or whatever your name is!

(Lights up on SPOON preparing for bed, putting on tinted complexion cream)

BOSCH: Is that how you operate? Toy with a man's affections—

SPOON: I assure you, I've said nothing to Mister Shanks that could—

BOSCH: Bugger Shanks, I'm talking about Hoother! Twas there on paper, sounding for the world like you're falling for him!

SPOON: Can't a woman be sincere?

BOSCH: Centuries men have been wondering that one! *(Now noticing)* What are you doing, putting on a minstrel show?

SPOON: Complexion cream for luminous skin.

BOSCH: It's just a little low is all. I mean, sending him specimens—that's good—but duping a man by pretending to be smitten— *(Grabbing wrists)* that's how you did it to me, eh Hetty?

SPOON: Stop calling me that! *(Heartsick)* And I'm not pretending.

(BOSCH assesses SPOON, then—)

BOSCH: *(Grinning)* Course you are. You haven't even met him. *(Grin fading as he gleans she's serious)* Or received a letter!

(SPOON sheepishly shrugs.)

BOSCH: You're not falling for him—you're falling for your own imagination!

SPOON: I don't care—it feels real enough.

BOSCH: Christ, it's like when you left me for that shank of a sailor!

SPOON: That wasn't me!

BOSCH: I knew you shouldn't have come here—a broken button's more reliable than you.

SPOON: What do you want from me.

BOSCH: Crack into that lamphouse, let me blow out the ember, and I'll let you live.

SPOON: Is that a threat?

BOSCH: It's a plea. I need you.

SPOON: How much do you need me? Now, ssh. It's my quiet time. *(Reaching for book)* We'll see if this doesn't send us to sleep.

BOSCH: *(To SPOON)* Whatcha got there?

SPOON: *(Reading cover)* "A History of Brood, by Vicar Enry Leap." Rats to history.

BOSCH: You can't run away from it, Hetty. The Past means something you know…

SPOON: Means something…or meant something?

BOSCH: Eh?

SPOON: *(To BOSCH)* Ssh.

(WICKER knocks and enters SPOON's room.)

WICKER: Pardon Miss, can I stay with you tonight?

(SPOON beckons WICKER in as she begins the below, and gently gestures for him to take a place next to her. He lies down with one of her pillows. We hear a brook, owl hoot, the flap of wings, and other mysterious night sounds. Lights dim slowly on all but SPOON—)

SPOON: …Owl's light…owl's night…
The mice are in the mill…
The babbling brook is babbling on,
And lord it lends a chill
For All of History's found within
The blather of that rill….
A stream of words, the sum of which
Adds up to naught but nil—
All that was and all that is

And all that ever will…
So sleep…sleep, my dear…sleep until—

(Suddenly BOSCH *screams with frustration, impatience, growing claustrophobia, in unison with* LEAP, *who has awoken from a nightmare screaming.* TOOM *rushes in)*

TOOM: Was that you, Vicar?

LEAP: A nightmare is all. I never felt so oppressed.

TOOM: You're still shaking.

LEAP: Twas awful. I dreamt…I was trapped in a coffin…with you.

TOOM: *(Climbing into* LEAP's *bed)* I've had terrible dreams as well.

LEAP: What are you doing? Get out of my bed!

TOOM: The dream started out alright—there was a pig, you see, dressed in German fashion—

LEAP: I'm feeling very oppressed!

TOOM: *(Snuggling)* Ah if only I was Mrs Nelles, eh Vicar?

LEAP: *(Changing subject, sternly—)* I'm changing the subject to that bell device. Why is it still up! I told you to take it down days ago.

TOOM: Well it's like this, Vicar. It's not coming down.

LEAP: I beg your pardon?

TOOM: She's only one away from her quota, and it's the last town on her tour!

LEAP: What did she offer you. *(More firmly)* What did she offer you.

TOOM: …well…for installing the bell device, and watching over it…she promised me a ten percent discount on any automata from the catalogue.

LEAP: I should have figured—

TOOM: So it's not fifteen groats for the pig and boot, tis only five, so I'm nearly there!

LEAP: Five? Where do you get five from?

TOOM: Fifteen minus ten.

LEAP: You said ten percent.

TOOM: Aye.

LEAP: Well it's not the same thing as ten. Ten percent of fifteen is— (*Calculates*) It's for thirteen and a half she's selling the pig, not five. Poor Mister Stoup—

TOOM: Get off me! So help me God, I'll get the groats somehow—

LEAP: I won't have any more of your graverobbing, if that's what you're thinking.

TOOM: Tis what I'm thinking.

LEAP: Well for God's sake, stop thinking it! You think that graveyard's just a lot of bones and mud?

TOOM: Aye.

LEAP: It's not. It's the meeting place of Past and Present—a landscape called Memory. Why do you think I was writing my cursed History of Brood? Cause without Memory, we're half-wits, and with it—

BOSCH: —we're buggered.

LEAP: —we're connected—with memory we're connected to our own lives, and the lives of all who have lived, thus making every plot in my kirkyard holy and inviolate!

TOOM: What a bucket of bollocks! There's gold pocket watches down there, and wedding rings, and we should take what we can cause, aye, the rest is just bones and mud, I seen it!

LEAP: Now you listen to me—I want you to stop your repugnant activities once and for all, do you understand? ...Do you understand?

(Same night. Lights up on HOOTHER *reading letter from* SPOON. *As* HOOTHER *and* SPOON *read letter,* SPOON, *still in complexion cream, jostles* WICKER *awake and sends him on his way to deliver, presumably, the letter we are now hearing.)*

HOOTHER: *(Reading)* "Dear Mister van Hoother... tonight I enclose nothing at all...

SPOON: *(As voice of the letter, distraught)* ...Or so it seems. But it's impossible not to enclose something. At the top of the page, you'll notice a word has smudged. I can't explain it, you've affected me most strangely, and a tear, of all things, has fallen onto the page. Surely you know that even within a single teardrop, a thousand creatures and countless more swim about, and live, and die... How absurd then if you say to yourself you're content inside your tower. Inside? Outside? Arbitrary. Meaningless. Nothing truly separates us—

(Suddenly, a scream from TOOM *and* BOSCH. *Same Night. Lights up on* TOOM *panting, backing away in horror from a recently re-opened grave, dropping spade)*

TOOM: *(To grave as he backs away)* Tis not possible!.... Ya...ya can't be—!...

*(*TOOM *hyperventilating, then notices* WICKER *[Who is returning from his postal errand] looking at him. He recovers enough.)*

TOOM: *(Threateningly)* A little late to be out and about, eh Grigs?

WICKER: *(Terrified)* I didn't—!

TOOM: *(Attention turning back to grave. shuddering)*
Christ that bastarding Lavender nearly sent the life out
of me…

WICKER: *(Terrified)* Y-y-you're digging her up!?

TOOM: Aye, nine years—time enough for the flesh to
melt, nick a ring off a finger— *(Shuddering again as
he looks toward grave)* …but that bloody bespectacled
girl…What do you think I saw when I opened the lid?

*(TOOM forces WICKER to look into open grave. WICKER
gasps.)*

TOOM: A face as fresh as morning staring back at me.
(Looking into grave) …Nine years dead and not a jot of
rottenness about her… *(Clutching WICKER tighter)* Why
Grigs?! Why won't she go away?!

WICKER: *(Terrified)* I don't know…

TOOM: *(Desperately searching for answer)* They say the
saints don't decompose. Tis possible? *(Pained)* –ah
you bastarding girl…twill have to be your whole
finger comin off to get that ring… *(Wielding knife under
WICKER's chin)* And if I hear any chat about me digging
up the dead—

WICKER: You won't!

TOOM: I'll find you, scoutie. And smear you cross this
parish like so much paint on a palette!

*(TOOM shoves WICKER to the ground. Lights snap up on
ARMITAGE and TRICITY, next day, lazily cloud-gazing,
picnic spread beside them. Birdsong, etc. And plums.)*

TRICITY: Armitage…

ARMITAGE: Yes, my peach?

TRICITY: *(Cloud-gazing)* Do you think of me even when
I'm not around?

ARMITAGE: *(Still cloud-gazing)* Out of sight, out of mind.

TRICITY: Armitage!

ARMITAGE: When you're out of my sight, I truly go out of my mind.

TRICITY: *(Kissing him)* Don't play with your words, Mister Shanks, it's rude.

ARMITAGE: *(Eating a plum)* Are you happy?

TRICITY: Awfully! Has there ever been a picnic like this one?

ARMITAGE: *(Brooding)* It's true…

TRICITY: What a goose you are. I'll never forget that moment I saw you drifting down the stream…and then you catching sight of me at my laundering—

ARMITAGE: Who knew you'd be out laundering so early?

TRICITY: And did you see the look on Spoon's face when we floated by her? It was priceless.

ARMITAGE: *(Feigning)* Oh? Did we pass her?

TRICITY: By the Fingle Bridge—I'm sure she wishes she could have boarded our little boat too.

ARMITAGE: Well…only to give us a pitch—

TRICITY: Yes, you a sales pitch, and me a pitch into the water— *(Assuming* SPOON's *voice)* "Oh Mister Shanks, I do hope you don't mind my tossing Miss Tiara into the drink, but I was so hoping I could catch you alone—"

ARMITAGE: *(Playing along)* "Be it an hour or a hundred evenings, Miss Spoon, my ear is here for you—"

TRICITY: *(As* SPOON*)* "Mister Shanks…I am asking you….for a moment…to trust me…"

(The interview becomes more intimate as they get caught up in the game, their lips drawing nearer.)

ARMITAGE: "Now now, Miss Spoon, I don't trust just anyone…"

TRICITY: *(Pouting seductively)* "Am I just anyone to you?"

ARMITAGE: "Oh if only you knew, Miss Spoon, how I truly felt—"

TRICITY: "How can I know how you truly feel without touching you. Everywhere."

ARMITAGE: "O then touch away!"

(And ARMITAGE and TRICITY kiss passionately. But she, coming to her senses, becomes disturbed by his increasing ardor.)

TRICITY: …stop…Armitage, stop…Armitage… Armitage!

(TRICITY struggles free. ARMITAGE momentarily bewildered, then, quickly—)

ARMITAGE: It's not what it looks like!

TRICITY: You were just kissing her! Madly!

ARMITAGE: I wasn't! I forgot it was you! I mean Miss Spoon! I mean, I mean—you trapped me!

TRICITY: I didn't! She just keeps popping up! *(Realization hitting)* Armitage, we're done for.

ARMITAGE: Don't say it! You know I can't be that close to you without—

TRICITY: Without what? Thinking of her? And what incenses me isn't that you love her—for we're free to love as we choose—but that you don't respect me enough to admit it!

ARMITAGE: *(Exasperated, on heels of previous line—)* Damn it, marry me, if you don't believe me!

TRICITY: *(In a temper)* I will marry you.

ARMITAGE: *(Just as impetuously)* Fine!

TRICITY: Fine!

*(*ARMITAGE *and* TRICITY *brood over their spat. And then, slowly realizing that it's not such a bad idea)*

TRICITY: I will marry you....

ARMITAGE: *(Half-hearing)* What?...

TRICITY: *(Louder, growing confident that it's a good idea)* I will marry you.

ARMITAGE: *(Confused, ill-at-ease)* You will?

TRICITY: *(Now beginning to beam, relieved and overjoyed)* O Armitage...I will! ...I will!...

(We hear music and festivities, softly at first, then louder. Lights up on public house, days later during the Engagement Celebration for ARMITAGE *and* TRICITY. NELLES *is out of her black crepe.* BOSCH, *with bottle, is passed out on the floor.)*

LEAP: A toast! I'd like to make a toast. First to Mrs Beautiful Mrs Nelles, who has graciously relented for this one night at least—this glorious night on which we gather to celebrate the engagement of our two lovers—to reopen her public house, and may the drink forever flow!

(General "here-here"s and clinking of glasses and bottles)

LEAP: And now to our Mister Shanks and soon to be Mrs Mister Shanks—we've waited a long time for this. Now I'm sozzled to be sure, but.... *(With tears in his eyes)* God bless you both! Now swish around—dance and keep dancing!

WICKER: *(Desperately trying to rouse* BOSCH*)* Mister Bosch! ...Please—put down the drinkin' —you've got to rouse yourself!

(*Lights up on* TRICITY *storming away from the publichouse.*
ARMITAGE *follows.*)

TRICITY: "Miss Spoon"! "Miss Spoon"! She's all you've
talked about all evening!

ARMITAGE: (*Appealing*) Darling—

(NELLES *comes out, carrying a wrapped package*)

NELLES: Oh here's where you two lovebirds are
hiding—

ARMITAGE: We were just coming in—

NELLES: I found one more gift behind the bench—

TRICITY: (*Eyes brightening*) Oh thank you!

ARMITAGE: (*Alarmed, he tries to grab package*) We'll open
it later—

TRICITY: (*Running away from* ARMITAGE, *laughing and
beginning to unwrap it*) No, let's do it now…I think I
know what it is….

ARMITAGE: (*Still alarmed*) It's needs a touch-up—

TRICITY: Always the perfectionist— (*She finally unwraps
it, but then must mask her shock*) ….Oh.

NELLES: What is it, dear?

TRICITY: (*Keeping it close to chest*) It's a portrait of…me…
by the stream… My darling's been working on it for
months…

(LEAP *comes out.*)

LEAP: Mrs Nelles! There you are!

NELLES: Look at you!

LEAP: Look at yourself, you giant peach tart! (*Pulling*
NELLES) It's back to the party with ya! (*Putting up fists
jokingly*) Or is it you're wanting another tussle!?

NELLES: (*Laughing*) Enry, honestly! Excuse us, dears….

(LEAP *and* NELLES *exit laughing.* TRICITY, *clearly shaken but trying to stay calm—*)

TRICITY: *(Showing him portrait, with tears)* This was meant as a gift to Her… In some private moment you actually painted over my face and put her's on instead!

ARMITAGE: Let's go inside.

TRICITY: Did you make any promises to her?

ARMITAGE: No—

TRICITY: Did she make any to you?

ARMITAGE: No—

TRICITY: Did you make love to her—

ARMITAGE: Stop it—

TRICITY: Just tell me. Cause I'll only imagine the worst if you say nothing. Are you in love with Miss Spoon… Armitage?…

(Long pause. The sounds of the celebration are audible in the distance)

ARMITAGE: I don't know.

TRICITY: Well…that's it then. She's in her room as we speak. You should go tell her.

ARMITAGE: I don't want to.

TRICITY: I insist. Go. Now….Please. Go!

ARMITAGE: My darling—

TRICITY: *(Now losing composure, crying as she runs off)* I'm glad you've found what you're looking for…

(A baleful jig's playing in the public house. BOSCH *is passed out with bottle.* TOOM *is absent.* WICKER, *in tears, tugs on* BOSCH's *sleeve desperately—*)

WICKER: *(Desperate crying)* Mister Bosch!

BOSCH: Stop tugging and go to the privy already!

WICKER: *(Desperate)* But I did go! And I saw...I—

BOSCH: *(Brushing him off)* I don't need the details!

WICKER: But twas awful! Open your eyes cause you're not noticin'—

BOSCH: *(Now noticing—)* What's going on there— Shanks is heading up the stairs...

WICKER: Our Mister Shanks...

ARMITAGE: I'm giddy...I'm sad...

BOSCH: *(Confused)* And he looks like bloody hell...

WICKER: Up the stairs he climbs...

TRICITY: With heady thoughts but heavy tread he climbs...

ARMITAGE: With hope and trembling heart I climb...O Miss Spoon—in the Book of Elopements, our names shall be writ at the very top!

(Music reaching climax—)

BOSCH: *(Suddenly sobering)* Wait a tick—somethin's not right—!

(And suddenly, from offstage, ARMITAGE screams. The music dismantles to chaos, as—)

ARMITAGE: *(Offstage)* O God! Help! Somebody! Come quickly! ...O No! ...O God! ...O God!...

(The sprawled corpse of Miss Spoon in nightgown and complexion cream revealed in dim light.)

END OF ACT ONE

ACT TWO

(Three Days Later [Friday])

(An impressionistic sound/music mix evoking the chaotic events that transpired after the end of ACT ONE—a jig dismantling, screams, sobs, slammed doors, hushed voices, solemn directions to lift a coffin, organ music, a spade in the dirt, dirt on top of the coffin, amidst more sobs, keening, etc. and possibly even the whispers and the "get in!"/"let me out!" of TOOM *and* SPOON *as mentioned by* TOOM *in his ACT TWO confession. 15-20 seconds total. Then lights up on assorted characters—)*

ARMITAGE: *(Devastated)* When I found her lying there, my own heart stopped…

LEAP: There was no pulsation, no respiration, no indication of life whatsoever.

NELLES: *(Back in black crepe, weeping)* A killing jar was discovered by her side. With the remnants of cyanide within.

TRICITY: Her death was proclaimed—

LEAP: Misadventure. An ill-conceived attempt to send herself to sleep. Case closed.

TOOM: And that very night her corpse was carried to the kirk —

LEAP: And over my most strenuous objections, she was buried—

BOSCH: —beneath her own bell device…

WICKER: *(Angry tears)* Why did you go and put her in the ground?! I loved her!

BOSCH: I've told you a thousand times, t'isn't me! Stories do what they do!

WICKER: But she'll be back, right? I mean, all she has to do is stop being dead after being dead!

BOSCH: Aye, and a snap, that is. If your name's Christ.

WICKER: But I thought you needed her to get into the lamphouse!

BOSCH: I do! *(Deep in concentration)* Died on a Tuesday, Buried on a Wednesday…

WICKER: …and yesterday was Thursday.

BOSCH: And the bell didn't ring.

WICKER: We just have to wait! Twill be part of the twist!

BOSCH: That bell could be sittin there silent til Johnny Pyot's Term Day!

WICKER: *(Determined)* She's coming back!

BOSCH: *(Erupting)* What happened to her!? What was she thinking!? What was she up to!? Why did she abandon us! *(Suddenly remembering)* …oh wait a tick… dear god…

WICKER: Whatcha thinkin?

BOSCH: I'm thinking bout Hetty with her skirts hitched up…. *(Seeing in mind's eye, seemingly salaciously—)* Aye…there ya go…

(Pause)

WICKER: Mister Bosch?

BOSCH: Twas at the tidepools—she said I'd be done with my questions if could open her box…. *(Lightbulb flash)* Holy Scamander! The strongbox!

(Lights up on LEAP, TOOM, *and* NELLES *in publichouse arguing. On the table, the sturdy-looking Bodum & Wattney strongbox.)*

NELLES: But it isn't ours to take! These are all the proceeds from her previous sales—

LEAP: The groats in this box can do a lot more good in Brood than in the pockets of Bodum and Wattney!

TOOM: But we'll be getting her in trouble!

LEAP: I would say her troubles go well beyond this box, Mister Stoup.

NELLES: *(Grieving)* Oh Enry, how could you be so insensitive?

TOOM: Besides, Vicar, she's coming back any moment now!

LEAP: No she's not!

TOOM: And when that bell rings, won't we all be lining up at her grave to order our Bodum and Wattneys!

LEAP: Wasn't it you spending the whole morn with this box trying to smash it?

TOOM: Oh I still think we could smash it.

NELLES: There'll be no more smashing.

TOOM: Dan the Smith could smash it.

LEAP: The woman says No Smashing!

TOOM: Sure, that's what she says—but as soon as our backs are turned, she'll sneck upstairs and look for the key!

LEAP: For the hundredth time, there is no key! You see? Five dials, each dial containing the letters of the alphabet—Tis a word, one five-letter word that opens the box, and nothing else.

TOOM: Nothing else but smashing it.

NELLES: *(Weeping)* Oh I never should have given her that poison…

LEAP: Now now—how were you to know…

NELLES: I still remember her last words as she went up those stairs—"I'm going to sleep tonight if it kills me."

LEAP: Oh that foolish woman—

NELLES: Yet I can't help thinking what she said about the killing jar. How sometimes beetles she thought were dead—

LEAP: *(Gritted teeth)* Look, I was against her being buried beneath the bell, but its silence has borne me out. She's dead. *(Pause)* Right…so now can I please hear the rest of what we've got?

NELLES: *(Reluctantly reads a piece of paper)* "Clock", "Prate", "latch", "clunk"—

TOOM: I thought of clunk.

NELLES: —"music", "filch"—

TOOM: Filch is mine.

LEAP: Keep quiet.

NELLES: — "drink", "mound", "piles"—

TOOM: I thought of piles.

LEAP: Well it didn't open the box so it doesn't matter!

TOOM: It mattered when I had 'em. They're a bad friend when you're trying to sit. Piles are.

LEAP: Thank you.

TOOM: And I didn't hear "ozle" on the list neither. Did you try "ozle"?

LEAP: Later. Read on.

NELLES: "Glint", "gleam", "sheep", and "dream".
That's all we have so far.

LEAP: *(Proud)* Not a bad run. How many is that,
altogether.

NELLES: Twenty-three.

LEAP: And how many combinations did she say were
possible?

NELLES: Eleven million.

(Profoundly dispirited pause, then—)

TOOM: I'm telling you, it's "ozle".

LEAP: I don't even know what that is.

NELLES: It's a cork buoy you attach to a herring net.

LEAP: Herring— Fine! How do you spell it.

TOOM: O-

LEAP: *(Manipulating dial)* O-

TOOM: Zed-

LEAP: Zed-

TOOM: L-

LEAP: L-

TOOM: *(The last letter)* E.

LEAP: E— *(He waits for* TOOM *to feed him the last letter,
then realizes—)* Oh for god's sake, it isn't even five
letters! Will you stop wasting our time!

TOOM: *(Erupting with unexpected emotion)* Go boil your
bonce! All she wanted to do was sell you a bell, you
gashing swasher, and now she's down in the ground
cause you were too bloody cheap! Well I'm telling you,
that bell's gonna ring today, do ya hear, it has to, or
else…oh christ…

(And TOOM, *clearly tortured, takes a bottle as he exits, and* BOSCH *who had been watching the scene discreetly despairs)*

BOSCH: *(Dazed)* Eleven million combinations…

WICKER: *(Innocently)* Do you think we'll try them all? Cause that might take a while.

BOSCH: *(Brooding)* I knew she was the devil. *(yet mystery niggles)* But she couldn't have misadventured on cyanide—I mean, that's just stupid.

WICKER: She survived the Typhoon of Frogs.

BOSCH: That she did! And the Flood of Blood. And the Hall of a Hundred Mirrors, remember that one? *(Half-hearted)* I mean you didn't see anything, did ya?

WICKER: *(Utterly terrified)* No! Nothing! I didn't see nothing at all! I didn't! No! Nothing!

(Beat)

BOSCH: Are you sure?

*(*WICKER, *utterly terrified, nods vigorously.)*

BOSCH: *(Impressed actually)* You are, hands down, the Lousiest Liar in the World. *(Threatening)* Now out with it—what do you know! Is she up to something? Was she murdered? Did she off herself? *(Out of patience)* Do you want to shackle me here for eternity!?

*(*WICKER *wants to tell, but something's keeping him back, resulting in anguished face and heavy breathing, and general squirming during interrogation…but no words. Finally—)*

BOSCH: *(Spitting towards him)* Get out of my sight!

LEAP: *(Trying to console)* This is all very difficult….

NELLES: *(In tears)* My daughter and now Miss Spoon. Two people I've personally done in…

LEAP: *(Gently)* Don't be ridiculous. *(Gentle joke)* You think I'd marry a murderess?

NELLES: *(Coldly)* I really don't know whom you'd marry.

LEAP: *(Chuckling nervously)* Well...I'd marry you of course.

NELLES: What are you talking about.

LEAP: *(Bewildered)* I asked you to be my bride and you said "yes"!

NELLES: *(LEAP's insane)* No I didn't.

LEAP: At the Engagement Celebration!

NELLES: *(Looking at fingers)* I don't seem to have a ring.

LEAP: Well...no... Rings are hard to come by here, what with our unrivaled poverty and all...

NELLES: But you wouldn't have proposed without one, would you? *(Tenderly)* Enry dear, you imagined it. You did have a lot to drink.

LEAP: *(Sarcastic of course)* Aye, and then I went and told the little men about our betrothal, and they were all so lovely—they took me back to Fairyland where we drank from buttercups and danced a jolly reel. *(Erupting)* I didn't imagine it!

NELLES: *(Firmly)* And I say you did.

LEAP: *(Perplexed/frustrated)* But—! ...Oh... But I mean, if... Well...so where do we stand?

NELLES: *(Appalled)* This is hardly the time for courting! Are you so unfeeling that a death to you means nothing but a chance at some groats and a little wooing on the side?

LEAP: I'm just trying to help the—

NELLES: Help would be going to that graveyard and disinterring my daughter.

LEAP: Are you not done with that nonsense?!

NELLES: Oh, nonsense is it?! She haunts me!

LEAP: *(Shrill)* Well tell her to stop haunting you!

NELLES: I want you out!

LEAP: Oh for God's sake—

NELLES: Out!

LEAP: Fine! But I'm taking that box with me!

NELLES: No you're not! Everything of Miss Spoon's stays right where it is.

LEAP: Then I'm not going anywhere.

NELLES: *(Putting up fists)* I'll drag you out.

LEAP: *(Putting up fists)* Oh I'm well-practiced wrestling women if that's what you're wanting. Now are we getting back to the list or what.

(Beat. Then NELLES finally relents with—)

NELLES: Idiot. *(Beat)* That's five letters.

LEAP: *(Staying calm)* That it is, Mrs Nelles.

NELLES: *(Writing on list)* Goes well with another one— "Vicar."

LEAP: *(Pleasantly)* Aye. And I just came up with one myself. "Widow." Also "dunce."

NELLES: *(Just warming up)* Oh well I've got another one, it's—

HOOTHER: Blink.

(Lights up on HOOTHER, checking his beacon. His jauntiness now seems a tad forced.)

HOOTHER: Good. Well Jarl van Hoother, we have all we need. New letters? No. Specimens? No. All we need— Our books, our tea, our never-varying view of the— *(He suddenly sees something on horizon. Color drains from face)* Great Rumphius and Fooks! *(He searches desk frantically, pushing things off desk, to find spyglass. Peers out with spyglass. He then searches frantically through stack of letters.)* Spoon's Letters. Number 3. No. Number— Ah! Letter One, Line 12— *(Reads)* "—expecting a ship to arrive in due time. I hear that here ships rarely if ever appear but this ship, sir, is a certainty.

HOOTHER/SPOON: *(Echoing voice only. Reading letter)* Do be Assured that I shall be boarding that ship when it docks, and the opportunity that has just knocked shall never knock again.

HOOTHER: *(Reading letter)* Please find enclosed...one bluebell..." *(Brooding, with burning eyes)* The first letter. Then all the letters that followed, followed by silence, followed by...a ship...Miss Spoon... *(Mood changing)* ...if you've given up then good riddance!

(WICKER, still with poorbox, is on hillock, a bluebell or two about, carrying ARMITAGE's portrait of SPOON)

WICKER: *(To portrait)* Mum, you've got to ring the bell cause I'm needing company in this uggsome place.... This is where I first saw you. I'll take a clump of grass the better to remember.

(Suddenly WICKER hears TOOM in the distance. Terrified, he drops portrait and looks for place to hide as TOOM sings. Desperate, WICKER stands stock-still hoping to pass for a tree.)

TOOM: *(In midst of singing)*
You replaced my eyes with a leaking pump
Twasn't very nice
You replaced my heart with a burning coal
I'd rather it was ice...
(Sees WICKER and stops singing) You've got something in your twigs, tree.

WICKER: *(With closed mouth, terrified, as tree)* No I don't.

TOOM: *(Prising out of WICKER's fist—)* A clump of grass. *(Violently interrogating)* Whatcha be doing with this?!

WICKER: *(Terrified)* Noothing!

TOOM: *(He pockets grass, then spots the portrait on the ground.)* And here's a nice trinkem—

WICKER: Don't touch it!

TOOM: *(Holding it up, demeanor changing to tenderness, as soon as he sees that it's—)* —Miss Spoon... O Anna... what happened to ya? *(Now aware of WICKER, and, threateningly—)* You know what happened to her Wick? Or are you needing some reminding...

WICKER: I'm not!

(TOOM looks furtively around, drags WICKER to an isolated spot where no one not even BOSCH can hear them.)

TOOM: What tricks the moon plays with her light, eh Wick? And the moon was out fierce that night...So tis conceivable twas a duck you saw, and not a man with a great suspicious sack aneath her window. *(He clutches WICKER by collar)* Say it!

WICKER: I saw a duck!

TOOM: Cause if I hear any chat putting me with her demise— *(But stops short, changes to a strange tenderness again)* ...dear christ...I don't want to harm no one no more...I can't look at a face without seeing the skull beneath the skin.... Do you think that bell's gonna ring, Grigs?

WICKER: ...I don't know....

TOOM: *(Growing sinister again)* Well I'll tell you this— keep your mooth shut or I'll flay you alive and string you up in a tree by your miserable breeks!

(And TOOM shoves WICKER to the ground and exits with the portrait.)

WICKER: "Breeks" are trousers. The wooden breeks is "the wooden trousers," and it's a coffin....a coffin.... *(Lowered voice, with dire conviction)* Inside the wooden

breeks, mother isn't dead but asleep. And when she
wakes up…she'll ring the bell. Please mum. Please
mum…

(Lights up on TRICITY'*s room.* TRICITY *is reading and*
ARMITAGE, *drunk and unkempt, holds a bottle and wilted*
flower. The room contains a sizable wooden hope chest—
conceivably the town privy on its side.)

ARMITAGE: Please my dewdrop—I don't miss her. It's
you that I'm missing.

(Pause. TRICITY *continues to read, so tries different tact—)*

ARMITAGE: Em…you're looking well.

TRICITY: *(Still not looking up from her book)* You look well
yourself Mister Shanks.

ARMITAGE: Well then looks deceive, for to me there
is no more Poetry in this world. It has fled from me.
(Then, because he can't help himself—) Like the ivory-
wingéd Pleiades from Orion.

TRICITY: *(Still reading book)* I'm sorry, did you say
something?

ARMITAGE: I have come for my personal effects. *(Trying*
desperately to unnerve her) My letters, my Keats…my
Keats, which I merely lent; I'm now asking for it back,
regardless of how much that book might mean to you.

TRICITY: *(Without looking up, non-chalantly)* It's on the
shelf.

ARMITAGE: *(Finding a box on the mantle)* What's in here?

TRICITY: Nothing.

ARMITAGE: Nothing to eat?

TRICITY: No.

ARMITAGE: *(Removing from the box—)* A key…

TRICITY: *(Finally looking up from book)* Put that back.

ARMITAGE: Would that it were a key to your heart.

TRICITY: If you're looking for your letters, Mister Shanks you shan't find them over there.

ARMITAGE: I'm looking for some sign of forgiveness from you.

TRICITY: Well Give It Up.

ARMITAGE: My starling—

TRICITY: Stop it.

ARMITAGE: My willow—

TRICITY: Oh is it a tree now? Did you know that in all your letters, you never mentioned my name?

ARMITAGE: Angel—

TRICITY: Tricity. I made a list of all the things I am, it's remarkable. *(Reading from her list)* Cuttlefish, primrose, an opera hat for god's sake—

ARMITAGE: But don't you see…You were the whole world to me—

TRICITY: But not Tricity. It was never love with us, just…just romance. It's Spoon you loved, or you wouldn't have left me for her!

ARMITAGE: It's not that simple!

TRICITY: *(Resuming list)* Lotus, laurel, hyacinth, robin, dove—

BOSCH: *(Brooding)* Aye, there's the question—cause it felt like it, but was it. Was it love, Hetty. Every bloody chapter of the bloody story predicated on the one simple and surely idiotic assumption that you loved us. That you'd claw your way through any amount of muck just to come back to us, rather than simply wash your hands of a runty bairn and fob him off on a tinker naïve beyond measure. Was it love? Or was I just a dupe? Should I have looked even harder for you when you went and vanished? You married that sailor, what the feck was that! But then other times you…and I…

HETTY: *(Reading page from book)* "Semper Eadem."

BOSCH: *(Correcting pronunciation haughtily)* Eádem. Tis Latin.

HETTY: Dead language.

BOSCH: Dead me arse. Means "always the same."

HETTY: Ah, the motto for your lovemaking.

BOSCH: I'll show you my motto, you cretin.

HETTY: *(Putting up fists)* You'll have to catch me first.

(BOSCH takes out a small book, sits down on the stone, and reads, as—)

BOSCH: *(Reading)* Oh the Bosches never run. We'd rather read.

HETTY: *(Approaching him sulkily)* Swasher. *(Pause. And now actually curious—)* So what's that you're reading then?

(BOSCH, without warning, reaches behind him and grabs her, pulling her down. A shriek of laughter from her, and amidst various kisses—)

HETTY: Just as I thought—the Bosches never read. They'd rather ravage. Hey, what are you doing now— that's strange.

BOSCH: I thought my motto was "always the same."

HETTY: *(Slyly)* Oh nothing's the same after I appear.

WICKER: *(Offstage, distantly)* Mister Bosch!

(The spell dispelled, HETTY recedes, as—)

BOSCH: *(To self)* Memories… If I had any sense, I'd drown them all like a sack of kittens…

(WICKER enters, weeping as he will.)

WICKER: Mister Bosch! Toom took my clump!

BOSCH: Your what?

WICKER: My clump of grass.

BOSCH: I'm sick to bloody death of yer pestering and Toom-took-my-grassing!

WICKER: *(Bitterly to self)* He'll never get everything. *(Triumphantly taking out small box from pocket)* I still have this.

BOSCH: Whatcha got there.

WICKER: Music box. *(Proudly)* A Bodum and Wattney.

BOSCH: When did she give you that?

WICKER: Engagement Celebration. She said "Axiom 54." Then she touched her nose. *(Sadly)* That was the last time I saw her…

BOSCH: *(Taking box)* A music box, eh? *(He winds it, then slowly opens the lid. Silence)* Well you're half-right. It's a box. What's Axiom 54— "Give out rubbishy gifts?"

WICKER: *(Defensively)* It did play music! All her boxes did. Her hat box. Her pill box. Her strongbox too. Twas lovely, that music.

BOSCH: Waitaminute. You saw her open the strongbox?

WICKER: More than once. She'd say "nothing's the same after I appear," then she'd open it.

BOSCH: *(Agog)* Don't tell me she was giving you a clue!

WICKER: *(Recalling)* "I'm dead, yet alive"—that was another one.

BOSCH: *(Ready to hit him, but excited)* Grigs! We have two clues! For opening the box!

WICKER: But how will opening the box bring her back?

BOSCH: It won't. She said if I could open her box I'd be done with my questions. Well question number one— "How in the sodding hell do I get that ember snuffed!?" So I don't know—maybe in that box it isn't groats at all but a key. To the lighthouse door. Or a magical snuffer—

WICKER: But Mister Bosch, I saw it. *(Shrugging)* It's just groats.

BOSCH: *(Bitter despair)* I should have known…that liar…

(WICKER suddenly notices something in the far distance and points—)

WICKER: What's that?

BOSCH: *(Without even looking)* Spoon's ship. Should be here soon enough.

WICKER: It's pretty.

BOSCH: Go away.

WICKER: *(A sudden idea)* Oo! And I will! With Mum! On that boat! I'll open the box and use the groats to buy a ticket!

BOSCH: You do that.

WICKER: *(About to go)* Oh—can I have my music box back?

BOSCH: *(Pocketing box, or making it disappear with sleight of hand)* You never had a music box.

WICKER: *(Appalled)* I did!

BOSCH: It was just a box—it never played music.

WICKER: It did!

BOSCH: Prove it!

WICKER: But you took it! *(With tears)* Why can't you let me keep anything!

BOSCH: *(Grabbing* WICKER *by throat)* Cause Life, bauchle, is the momentary difficulty when swallowing your slaver...

*(*WICKER *gulps.)*

BOSCH: ...and it's gone.... Now leave me alone....

WICKER: *(With tears, hatefully)* My box did play music... and it was lovely...I know cause I remember... You can take my box... *(Running away)* but still I remember the music...!

(We hear TRICITY's *voice fade up as lights fade up on* ARMITAGE *and* TRICITY *in her bedroom.* TRICITY *is still reading from her list.* BOSCH *wanders over to the scene.)*

TRICITY: *(Faint to louder)* —I'm also a "music box," a "porpoise"; a "wooden drinking cup"—

ARMITAGE: Yes. All right. You've made your point.

TRICITY: So I trust you can see why I burned them.

ARMITAGE: *(Gasps)* Not every letter, surely—

TRICITY: Nothing but ashes now...

ARMITAGE: *(Devastated)* Then do you think, Phoenix-like, from out of those ashes our love can arise renewed?

TRICITY: Em...no. So... *(Waving)* Tinkerty tonk.

ARMITAGE: This can't be the end! *(Desperate, pointing)* What about that hope chest—you said it was intended for our future!

TRICITY: But we agreed we wouldn't think about our future, so I always kept it empty!

ARMITAGE: Then use it for our past! Keep our memories locked safe inside, where the moths may never get at them—

(*Lights quickly down on* ARMITAGE *and* TRICITY *and up on*
HOOTHER *studying. Every so often he looks up to check on
the ship's progress*)

HOOTHER: "Clothes moth!, lepidoptera, (*Looks up, down*)
larvae known for gnawing through whole wardrobes
of trousers... (*Looks up, down, resumes reading*) —The
pupa— (*Looks up, down*) The pu— (*Erupts*) How
does anyone expect me to concentrate with that
ship wingling in front of me! (*Violently turning to—*)
"Clothes moths, methods of removing"!

(*Lights up instantly on* ARMITAGE *and* TRICITY—
ARMITAGE *sitting defiantly in hope chest*)

TRICITY: Get out of my chest, Mister Shanks.

ARMITAGE: No.

TRICITY: You're drunk.

ARMITAGE: From your intoxicating presence.

TRICITY: (*Losing patience*) From the whiskey.

ARMITAGE: From the fortnights without food I've
endured.

TRICITY: Well you won't find anything to eat in there.

ARMITAGE: (*Bending down, rummaging in chest*) Then
what's this foie de veau doing in your picnic basket?

TRICITY: What picnic basket?

ARMITAGE: —a cold collation of smoked meats—

(*Subliminally, we begin to hear water lapping against a
docked boat*)

ARMITAGE: —scones with Devon cream—

TRICITY: Why must you make things so difficult—

ARMITAGE: Sparkling wine of our favorite vintage, a
raised pigeon pie—

TRICITY: I don't understand—you spent all that money on that picnic...and all for me?

ARMITAGE: *(With deepest sincerity)* I loved you.

TRICITY: And how I loved you!

ARMITAGE: And yes, you said yes, and all the world was ours....

(ARMITAGE beckons, and TRICITY, relenting, moves closer to the cedar chest)

TRICITY: Understand I'm quite aware—

ARMITAGE: Watch your step—

TRICITY: —that there isn't anything to eat in this chest.

(TRICITY sits and ARMITAGE begins to row. Sound of water more pronounced)

ARMITAGE: The food could wait, until we reached Ruesdael's Bluff. And then the plums—

TRICITY: The fresh plums... *(Lights begin to dim)* ...Oh dear...I'm not sure I like this.

ARMITAGE: *(Handing her a parasol)* Your úmbrell, Madam.

(In dim light, ARMITAGE rows, as if an automata, and TRICITY holds parasol behind her.)

BOSCH: *(Watching ARMITAGE and TRICITY tableau)* This could very well be the picture of Every Couple in Coupledom—one going forward, one going backward, and neither going anywhere at all. *(Looking up at HOOTHER)* Just like that bastard up there, going nowhere at all and thinking about nothing but—

HOOTHER: Molluscs! Actinia mollusca miss spoon and blanus. Good. *(Sips tea, and jauntily—)* Now let us name the ten subclasses of family *vertiginacea*— *(He rapidly counts with fingers) Ena, vallonia, acanthinula, miss spoon, clausilia, balea, marpessa, abida, lauria, columella, pupilla.*

(Pause. Looks at fingers) That's eleven. Something is wrong…. Take it slowly—Ena, vallonia, acanthinula, miss spoon— *(Stops short)* Ah. *(He has found the problem, perturbed. Pulls self together.)* Move on. Flowers! And the Sexual System for Classification as Devised by Linnaeus. *(Lingers perturbedly)* The sexual system. *(Clarifies)* For flowers. *(Considers as if for first time)* Sex. *(Clarifies)* The number of pistils, that is. *(Insistent)* Sex. *(Angry intensity)* Bluebells! *(Grabs clean sheet of paper, dips pen in ink, and says in a rush—)* Dear Miss Spoon crack open a new folio of the Ferguson and Ives and one can expect to find a diagram, an excellent diagram, of campinula rotundifolia, or rather, a bluebell, or rather, a campinula rotundifolia is a bluebell, ergo a diagram of a campinula rotundifolia is a diagram of a bluebell but Miss Spoon…. *(With ache in the heart)* …they were just diagrams… This *(Holding up dried bluebell)* is…a bluebell…and this…this…*flash.* Crack open, Cracked open a new folio, appendix 63 stroke K and found…inside… *(Holding up bluebell)* …this. *(Pained)* And all the excellent diagrams, rich with color and life, suddenly…and all the years of patient and meticulous study…all suddenly…as light…as slight… as paper. And so, and yet, I am writing to ask you… why your letters have suddenly…stopped… *(Dropping anguish)* …not that I care. I am writing to inform you that a ship, no doubt your ship…has been spotted… and…and I am simply writing actually to remind you to…leave…when you leave… To get out…to get out of my brain! …get out of my—

BOSCH: *(Considering* HOOTHER *at foot of lighthouse, hitting head)* Brain—you've been letting me down! How could I have missed it—Hoother doesn't know Spoon's dead! She's under the ground and still at work for us, for tis her silence that could very well tease him out his door! *(Excitedly planning)* And like a cat waiting for a mouse, I'll pounce as soon as the door swings open. A few good kicks, scamper up, blow out that blasted ember, and hey presto, done for good with this turd of a tale and beating the head against impossible puzzles left by impossible women!

*(Lights up on publichouse—*NELLES, LEAP, TOOM, *and* WICKER. *Night falling. Heavy rain outside.* NELLES *is reading latest entries to list—)*

TOOM: Did we try "ozle"?

LEAP: Shut up.

NELLES: *(Reading)* …drune…scrab—

WICKER: I thought of scrab.

LEAP: Stop interrupting.

TOOM: Besides, it's a lie, Vicar—I thought of scrab!

LEAP: It doesn't matter!

TOOM: *(To* GRIGS*)* And I thought I told you to beat it—

NELLES: He's no other place to go. And he has given us two clues.

LEAP: "I'm dead, yet alive" —

WICKER: —and "nothing's the same after I appear."

TOOM: How do we know the little scrunt's not making it up?

WICKER: She loved me!

TOOM: She didn't care tuppence for you.

WICKER: *(Bitterly, through tears)* Then why would she give me this!

(And WICKER *holds up a sheet of paper)*

LEAP: What do you have there, lad.

WICKER: *(Now fearful)* Nothing! Just a letter from Miss Spoon—

TOOM: Give me that! *(Snatching it away and reading first line)* It's not even addressed to you—it's meant for Jarl van!

WICKER: *(Snatching it back)* No it's not.

LEAP: Now, lad, tell us true.

WICKER: She gave it to me…to give to Jarl van….but then she…died….so I kept it.

LEAP: And will you let us read it?

WICKER: No.

NELLES: It isn't ours to read, Enry.

TOOM: *(To* NELLES*)* Oh come on, Polly Pious— *(And pointing to* WICKER*) —he's* read it already.

WICKER: I haven't! I swear!

TOOM: You expect us to believe that!?

WICKER: I don't know how to read!

TOOM: Right, that's it, you little urf—

*(*TOOM *lunges for letter, and* WICKER *tries to swallow it.)*

NELLES: You leave him alone!

*(*TOOM *rips it from his mouth, but* WICKER *ends up swallowing a small piece.)*

TOOM: He took a bite out of it!

NELLES: *(Firmly, and taking letter)* Probably the first solid food he's had all week.

(As NELLES *considers letter—)*

TOOM: Look at your eyes gleaming—you can't wait to read it.

*(*NELLES, *half-reluctantly, unfolds the letter and reads—)*

NELLES: *(Reading)* "Dear Mister van Hoother… This is the last note you shall receive from me. Before morning

I will be discovered dead..." *(She becomes distressed.)* Oh good god...how could she have known unless—

LEAP: *(Shaken)* She took her own life...

WICKER: She couldn't!

LEAP: Oh dear christ...

NELLES: *(Resuming reading, shaken)* "You've driven me to it... Tonight at least, I'll have a respite from your blink..."

LEAP: She hadn't slept, she wasn't thinking right—

NELLES: But to take your own life—

LEAP: *(With an arm around her for comfort)* Read on, dear.

NELLES: "I know you think by keeping aloof from people, you stand a chance of achieving a happiness elusive to the rest of us... But I'll tell you this—the gnaw in the stomach—

NELLES/SPOON: *(Voice only)* —at the thought of being buried alive—

SPOON: *(Voice only, echoing)* —comes not from the thought of starving to death, or running out of air... no...it's the knowing, like you've never known it before...that you're alive...you're alive while the rest of the world, oblivious, goes on without you... Is this not proof then that that which binds our souls to each other...that engagement, that Trust...is Life itself...

NELLES/SPOON: *(Voice only)*It's no wonder you're not interested in my product.

NELLES: *(Continuing to read letter)* But I am asking you, for a moment, to trust me. I'll show my trust in you, I'll tell you a secret. I know a word. *(She's growing more excited, hardly believing she's reading—)* A five-letter word I'm not supposed to tell a soul. But I'll tell you."

TOOM: Holy Scamander!

LEAP: Lord Harry!

NELLES: *(Reading with more excitement)* "It's a word both dead and alive—"

LEAP: I can't believe it!

NELLES: "Nothing's the same after it appears."

LEAP: God of Mercy!

TOOM: Keep quiet!

NELLES: "It's a word often difficult to say, and difficult to hear. It's the cause of sadness and the vanquisher of sadness."

TOOM: But what is it?! What's the bloody word!

NELLES: "Can you guess it? Of course you can. It's *(Beat,for a piece is missing)* …Forever more, and never more, Miss Spoon."

TOOM: Eh? I missed it.

LEAP: I missed it too. What was the word?

NELLES: I don't know…there seems to be a small piece missing from the page.

LEAP: What are you talking about?

(Beat, then a realization as they all turn to WICKER. *Beat)*

WICKER: *(Bewildered)* What? What did I do?

TOOM: *(Lunging)* Don't worry Vicar, I'll just rip the piece out of him!

NELLES: Mister Stoup, there will be no violence, now sit down!

TOOM: *(Very contrite and sincerely so)* You're right… there's no place for that—I'm turning over a new leaf…

LEAP: Come here lad… It's all right….

*(*WICKER *timidly approaches.* LEAP *grips him by the shoulders, trying to be gentle)*

LEAP: Do you know what you've done, lad? (*Now, less restrained*) Do you know what you've done, lad? (*Desperate and violent*) Do you know what—

TOOM: (*Pulling* LEAP *back from* WICKER) Easy Vicar! Easy! No violence, now, remember?

NELLES: Come here Wicker. Don't be afraid…

(WICKER *makes his way over to* NELLES, *who hands him a bedpan*)

NELLES: Do you know what this is used for.

WICKER: Bedpan.

NELLES: Now I want you to take this and go to the town privy, and don't come back again til you have something to show us. All right? Now get on with it.

TOOM: (*Encouragement/threat*) Master Grigs…we're with you all the way…

LEAP: (*Hand on* WICKER's *shoulder*) You're still young, lad, but this might turn out to be the most important bowel movement of your life.

(WICKER *nods, opens door, considers rainy weather, the thunder*)

TOOM: Jump up and down as you're walking—do a little dance—twill get things moving.

LEAP: Aye that's good advice. (*Sending him off*) Now blow.

(WICKER *exits,* LEAP *turns back to* NELLES *and* TOOM *and reassures—*)

LEAP: The air will do him good.

(*Briskly, lights up on* HOOTHER *at desk. He suddenly decides—*)

HOOTHER: And indeed. (*He stands up abruptly*) Why not go outside and stretch the legs a little.

BOSCH: *(Eagerly playing the other side of* HOOTHER'*s conscience)* Yes, why not.

HOOTHER: *(Sitting back down)* Because we can't abandon the flame, that's why not.

BOSCH: Hang the flame! It can burn without us for an hour.

HOOTHER: Our books tell us all we need to know of the world.

BOSCH: Does it tell us the smell of hay, the sway of branches, the wet of rain—

HOOTHER: Yes, in a hundred and twelve plates.

BOSCH: Hang the plates! We're talking about life!

HOOTHER: Hang life! We're talking about a woman!

BOSCH: And what if we are. She said she could make us happy.

HOOTHER: Happy!? Get one thing absolutely clear— It was not and is not and will never be my desire to be happy!

BOSCH: And now you just sound stupid.

HOOTHER: You're right. *(Getting up)* A quick stroll, what's the harm. To the staircase!

BOSCH: *(Rubbing hands, pleased at breakthrough in story)*

There we go! Now we've got that bespectacled rascal!

(And lights up on ARMITAGE *and* TRICITY, *still in the chest,* ARMITAGE *still rowing)*

ARMITAGE: It's funny, I'm not even hungry anymore—

TRICITY: Nor I. I remember it all—

ARMITAGE: You smelled so clean—

TRICITY: Your suntanned arms around me— Oh Armitage… It was nice, wasn't it…when She wasn't in the picture—

ARMITAGE: (*Dearly sincere*) Yes, it was…and all the delicacies of the world procured for her mean less than a crumb when you and I can feast our eyes upon each other, or drink in each other's gazes. When "O though banquets I've savoured, nothing tastes sweeter—"

TRICITY: "—than your lips."

ARMITAGE & TRICITY: Tennyson.

(ARMITAGE AND TRICITY *kiss passionately, but a thought suddenly occurs to her, and she breaks away.*)

TRICITY: …You said "all the delicacies of the world… procured for *her*…."

ARMITAGE: What, my goose?

TRICITY: (*Standing up as realization grows*) There I was washing clothes by the banks—I didn't know I'd be there just then…so how could you?

ARMITAGE: Wait.

TRICITY: (*Now becoming sure*) You were expecting Her— she was there waiting by the bridge!—

ARMITAGE: (*Sinking into the box*) No darling, honestly—

TRICITY: You bastard—if you love her so much, why aren't you with her now?!

ARMITAGE: (*Confused*) She's under the ground…

TRICITY: Precisely! (*She slams lid of the chest and sits on top of it*)

ARMITAGE: (*From inside chest*) Tricity, for god's sake!

TRICITY: You've raped my memories!

ARMITAGE: (*Urgently*) Look, whatever you do, do not lock this chest.

TRICITY: (*Spitefully locking the chest*) I'll do nothing of the sort.

ARMITAGE: *(Panicked)* You mustn't lock it, for I have the key.

TRICITY: *(Suddenly worried)* Didn't you put it back?

ARMITAGE: You...didn't lock this chest....

TRICITY: I did.

ARMITAGE: You didn't lock this—!

TRICITY: Why must you turn everything into an argument?! I did!

ARMITAGE: *(Panicked)* But I can't breathe!

(He begins screaming)

TRICITY: Don't panic, I'll go get help!

ARMITAGE: No, don't leave me! I beseech you! Get me out of here! Help!

(And now we also hear Hoother, as we see lighthouse door tugged upon and not budging)

HOOTHER: *(Intense panic)* Help! Help!

BOSCH: *(As Hoother's conscience)* Go over it again. Did you turn the handle?

HOOTHER: *(From behind door)* Yes!

BOSCH: You need to unbolt the door first.

HOOTHER: I unbolted it!

BOSCH: And—

HOOTHER: It didn't budge!

BOSCH: What do you mean it didn't budge!

HOOTHER: The door must have rusted shut from years of unuse!

BOSCH: A sound deduction.

HOOTHER: Thank you. And now here's another one. I'm trapped.

BOSCH: Don't panic.

HOOTHER: True. This tower was a vast and airy place just moments ago... Nothing has changed except a little bit of knowledge.

BOSCH: Exactly.

HOOTHER: The knowledge that I'm trapped. I'm trapped! Help!

ARMITAGE: Help! I can't breathe!

HOOTHER: Get me out of here!

(TOOM, LEAP, *and* TRICITY, *enter her bedroom with assorted tools*)

LEAP: Don't fear, Mister Shanks, we'll have you out in a twink.

TRICITY: Hold tight, darling!

(*Chest lid is flung open with crowbar. Silence. Long pause with characters in tableau*)

LEAP: ...oh dear...

TOOM: Not a bad trick.

TRICITY: (*Baffled*) I...I assure you he was here.

(*As all three look about the chest and room, bewildered—*)

LEAP: Well there must be some logical explanation...

TOOM: Why.

LEAP: Because the world is logical, Mister Stoup.

TOOM: If you say so.

LEAP: I do say so. I don't think so. But I say so.

TRICITY: (*Frantic*) He's gone and yet there's nowhere that he's not— Wasn't it here that we kissed? Wasn't it here that we fought? Who'd have thought my Love, locked tight in my hope chest, could ever disappear? Armitage?! Where have you gone?!

(HOOTHER, *either standing on chair or bent underneath desk, searching*)

HOOTHER: Where have you gone you blasted—Ah! *(He finds large book and blows off great quantity of dust. Reads title with disdain—)* "The Lighthouse Keeper's Companion." *(Turning pages, shaking head)* It's come to this. *(Finding—)* Here we are. Rust. *(Reading)* "The lighthouse keeper must keep a vigilant"—yes, yes, I know—"corrosion, moist salt air, oxidation...." Ah! "Lubricants!" *(Reads)* "One lubricant alone can undo the effects, if temporarily, of iron well-rusted."

BOSCH: Oil.

HOOTHER: *(He shuts book and looks about desk)* Oil? The only oil we have is the teaspoon's-worth of whale oil currently furnishing our lighthouse with light.

BOSCH: Well what's the problem? It's oil, we just need to get it—

HOOTHER: —and to get it all we have to do is snuff the light. *(Beat)* Thereby snuffing the only life we've known. Forever. That's the problem.

(WICKER, *with desperate pained expression, hands and teeth clenched, is running awkwardly in place in attempt to speed bowel progress. Stops to assess progress, detects none, begins routine again—still wearing poorbox, mind*)

BOSCH: *(Looking up at HOOTHER)* I had him. I was this close.

WICKER: *(While doing his dance)* So Hoother's not coming out?

BOSCH: He's as lodged in that lighthouse as... *(Now looking at WICKER's dance)* ...as, say, a priceless piece of paper in one's bottom.

WICKER: Mister Bosch, you've got to help! They'll kill me if I don't give up the word!

BOSCH: How do you expect me to help? It's a one-man job if ever I've seen one. Besides, I'm trying to squeeze out the answer to me own puzzle.

WICKER: What puzzle is that?

BOSCH: "A brief but unavoidable errand," that's what. That's what your mum said. Well it's been three thousand days and counting. Can that still be considered "brief"?

WICKER: No.

BOSCH: Well not so fast fellow. Rocks. Billion years and more some rocks have been sitting around. Three thousand days to, say, a piece of slate…tis barely a blink.

WICKER: But moother wasn't a piece of slate.

BOSCH: Now "unavoidable" —that's the word that stopped me in my tracks at the time. I couldn't very well ask your mother to avoid the unavoidable, could I? Especially if it's going to be "brief"!

WICKER: *(Dancing miserably)* Mister Bosch, you've gone over this before.

BOSCH: *(Ignoring* WICKER*)* And last we come to "errand". A little task, that's what errand means. But was it at her own behest… *(Mysteriously)* or another's? *(Impatient and irate)* Did she have to go and pick up a cabbage for an auntie for instance?! *(Angrier)* Was she running off to join your father, whether in the Hebrides or Hell!?, was she just a great fat cowardly liar, and she knew it wasn't a little task at all but an escape?!… That's my question, that's what I'd like to know, that's what I DEMAND to know, and that's what I'll…what I'll never know…so why do I keep asking! Every time I've swallowed this cud once and for all, bang, my stomach sends it back up for me to munge upon once again… And look what it's turned me into!

WICKER: You're dull.

BOSCH: *(Aghast at truth)* I'm dull! I could win a dullness contest against Mister Dull and his piece of brown paper! *(Rams his shoulder hard against* HOOTHER's *door, trying to open it. Groans—)* And I'm hurting myself! *(Turning fiercely on* WICKER*)* And I'm stuck in this blasted story cause you won't let me go!

WICKER: *(Blurting)* I'll let you go!

BOSCH: What?

WICKER: *(Softly)* I'll let you go. Go. I doon't want you to hate me anymore. Just Go.

*(*BOSCH, *dumbfounded for moment, and then—)*

BOSCH: *(Quite pleased)* And I will!— *(Now hesitating)* Cause you're doing all right…I mean, you're making out, you're making do—

WICKER: I'm hungry. And it's terrible, at night, when I'm alone, it gets the worst.

BOSCH: *(Actually hearing Grigs for once)* Well aye, that can be hard….

WICKER: I don't mind the baistings so much, but I sleep in a ditch and it's cold.

(As they stare at each other, we hear, fading up, a slightly-altered memory from top of ACT ONE)

HETTY: *(V O)* …Ah now, sometimes you just forget how to treat others. That's what makes you a poor tinker….

BOSCH: *(Softly correcting)* It's thinker.

WICKER: What?

BOSCH: I'm a poor thinker.

WICKER: *(Confused)* What are you saying? Go already!

BOSCH: Well.... *(A little embarrassed that he isn't leaping away)* Well the thing of it is...a story is like...a movement of the bowels...You can't very well just get up and leave midway...no...it demands you persevere and see it through...

WICKER: *(Confused)* You mean—

BOSCH: —by all that's holy, *(Pointing to lighthouse)*, that glim's getting snuffed and that keeper's getting his nose-specks crammed down his throat!

WICKER: You know who else wears nose-specks? Lavender.

BOSCH: Aye, that's grand. Now get back to your— *(A thought, remembering—)* ...You saw Lavender in the grave, didn't ya...

WICKER: *(Suddenly terrified he said something he shouldn't have)* I didn't!

BOSCH: *(Thinking hard)* Sure you did. "With a face as fresh as morning" staring back at you...And at the Engagement Celebration...you went out to use the privy and when you came back you were screwed up in fright. "Was it a ghost in the privy?" I said and you said, "no, twas aneath her window"—

WICKER: I didn't!

BOSCH: I'm done with your didnts! Now tell me what you saw!

WICKER: *(Blurts)* I saw a duck.

BOSCH: And nothing else?

WICKER: *(Squirming)* I saw a duck. *(Beat)* In a sack.

BOSCH: A sack? *(Puzzle coalescing more)* A sack big enough for, say, a dead person-sized duck!?

(WICKER, terrified, nods slowly.)

BOSCH: *(Dismissing* WICKER *and straining brain to put it all together)* Spoon went to bed every night in that complexion cream…Lavender was about her height, build—Grigs!—just what is Axiom 54?!

WICKER: What?

BOSCH: When she gave you the musicbox—she said "Axiom 54" and touched her nose!

WICKER: *(Dutifully)* "A demonstration is worth a thousand words."

BOSCH: …And that was the last thing she said to you?! —"A demonstration is worth…". *(Slapping forehead)* Dontcha see!? It wasn't suicide, and it wasn't misadventure—twas a first-class, take-them-all-in publicity stunt!

(Lights up on a tortured-looking TOOM *alone in graveyard)*

TOOM: And when that bell rings, won't we all be lining up at her grave to order our Bodum and Wattneys! She said she'd split her bonus commission for making her quota. And I'd have had that pig and boot with change to spare. Lord they're all gneeps and idiots—Shanks, that bloody idiot—

BOSCH: *(Putting it together, excitedly)* —had one look at the corpse, then ran screaming from the room.

TOOM: And Leap—that bloody idiot—

BOSCH: The woman he pronounced dead was dead, but that woman wasn't Miss Spoon….

TOOM: O Grigs, you bloody idiot…

BOSCH: *(To* TOOM*)* Wicker saw you with a sack on a ladder, but the corpse in the sack wasn't Spoon, it was Fanny Nelles' daughter—uncorrupted, and fitted out in Spoon's nightgown and complexion cream. And Leap, in the dark of that room never twigged it!

TOOM: Mrs Nelles, you bloody idiot—

BOSCH: A killing jar was placed by the bed and she thinks Spoon's death is all her doing…

TOOM: Twas working like a charm!

BOSCH: But it doesn't make sense. It's been three days—if it was a publicity stunt, then why—

TOOM: Why hasn't it rung!?

BOSCH: *(Becoming clearer)* Toom the Stoup—

TOOM: *(Tortured)* —bloody bloody idiot… Ring, for Chrissake! O Anna— Twas working like a dream, carrying Lavender to the kirk, you hiding in the shadows til I gave the all-clear, and you stepped into your coffin with the grace of a queen! But then you had second thoughts, and I was drunk— "Get in," I said. "Let me out," you said. And before you could say anymore—I didn't mean to slam the lid so hard. Out like a light you went, but you had said you hadn't slept for a week so I thought nothing of it…

BOSCH: …but now it's been too long…

TOOM: Anna Livia, I didn't mean it!

BOSCH: …you murdered her…

TOOM: *(Weeping)* …I live in a graveyard…the world is a graveyard! …Ring! ….Ring, you bloody… Ring!…

BOSCH: So there we are. She's gone. Dead by the gravedigger's hand.

WICKER: *(With great tears)* You can't believe that, Mister Bosch! You can't!

BOSCH: *(Looking* WICKER *in the eye)* And I won't. I won't leave it like this—I'll make it right, I swear.

*(*BOSCH, *roused, heads towards public house)*

WICKER: *(Calling out)* She has to come back!

*(Lights up on publichouse—*NELLES, TRICITY, LEAP. BOSCH *watches discreetly.)*

TRICITY: *(Looking out window)* It's getting dark out.

LEAP: *(Consoling to* TRICITY*)* Mister Shanks will be back.

TRICITY: *(Quite sure)* No. He won't.

NELLES: And that bell isn't going to ring today, is it.

LEAP: *(Gently)* No. It won't. That bell will always be silent. *(Resolved)* But will you not consider how new life can bloom…when the sound of a bell is silent.

NELLES: What are you on about, Enry—

TRICITY: When is the sound of a bell ever silent?

LEAP: When the ring… *(Takes ring out of pocket)* …is for your finger. Tis a vale of tears, this world, but surely some of those tears can be from happiness… *(On bended knee)* Mrs Nelles…Fanny…I love you…Will you marry me.

NELLES: *(Moved, looking at ring)* Oh Enry…I don't know what to say…I. *(Suddenly her eyes widen, she stumbles backward onto the ground.)*

LEAP: *(Greatly alarmed)* Fanny! Are you all right!?

NELLES: *(Ghostly pale)* That ring! Where'd you get it?

LEAP: From…around…you know…

NELLES: TIS LAVENDER'S RING!

LEAP: *(Truly surprised)* What?!

NELLES: The one she was buried in! *(Outraged beyond words)* You…you dug her up!?! So you could propose to me?!!

LEAP: *(Bewildered)* No! God No! I—Toom the Stoup— *(Quickly thinking up a lie)* …I disinterred your daughter…em…without telling you…to investigate your claim, and yet spare you from what is never not a distressing sight…em…and am relieved to report… yes…that Lavender was not buried prematurely…And, em, I took the ring as proof that I'm not just making it up.

(Beat. Then NELLES, *with profound relief—)*

NELLES: *(Tears)* Oh praise the bloody Lord...I never thought I'd find solace in hearing that my daughter was dead...but you say she was?... *(Profound gratitude)* Thank you Enry. Thank you. *(Beat)* Though I'm not sure if proposing to me with her ring shows the best judgment—

LEAP: *(Fumbling)* Well...I—

NELLES: At any rate, the answer's "no."

LEAP: What?

NELLES: Sorry dear. I won't marry you.

LEAP: *(Devastated)* But...you did say "yes" the first time.

NELLES: I thought we agreed you imagined it.

LEAP: I didn't imagine it! And that was the second time. I'm talking about the first time! *(Stomping)* Why did you marry that blasted sailor in the first place!?

NELLES: You mean Benjilum!?

LEAP: You had promised yourself to me! And then you turned round and married him—

NELLES: Well, it's in the past, isn't it.

LEAP: That's easy for you to say!

TRICITY: This is all a bit awkward isn't it.

LEAP: Damn it, am I getting an explanation or do I have to stand here all day!

NELLES: *(Firing right back)* With conduct like that?! No—you're not getting one!

(Pause)

LEAP: *(Restrained)* Yes…you're right…You owe me nothing…Forgive me, both of you…

*(*LEAP *exits in pain and encounters* TOOM. BOSCH *watches—)*

TOOM: Hey, so Vicar, how'd it work—with the ring and all. Did you sling her the question?

LEAP: *(Containing anger and pain)* Well, seeing as I proposed to her with the ring belonging to her buried daughter—

TOOM: *(Gasping)* Oh bloody hell! Vicar! I'm so sorry! I didn't do the math!

LEAP: What math did you have to do!!? *(Then giving up)* Oh it serves me right, asking my graverobbing gravedigger if he had any rings lying about….

TOOM: So can I have the ring back?

LEAP: No, she kept it.

TOOM: What?!

LEAP: Well it was her daughter's ring!

TOOM: Only cause I gave it to her!

LEAP: What are you talking about. *(Then realizing)* No… You were Lavender's mystery suitor? But…but she never left the house!

TOOM: She'd sneck out the window at night and meet me up on the hill. *(With great admiration)* Lord what a lunie lass she was… She'd have loved that pig and boot. I was buyin' it in her memory. Such nights we had…quiet, you know…though a little on the airish side… *(Sheepish)* Actually…that's probably how her cough came about…

LEAP: Oh god, that figures—Lavender died cause she was out with you….

TOOM: Well that's what I thought, Vicar—for years it tortured me! But digging her up, I was afforded a strange bit of solace, for I noticed…well, her legs. *(Long pause)* They were crossed.

LEAP: *(Shocked beyond measure)* What?

TOOM: We didn't put her in the ground like that.

LEAP: But…oh no…oh god…I'm going to be sick…

BOSCH: *(Seizing on* TOOM's *words)* Lavender was down there screaming and no one could hear her…It could have gone the same for our salesman, but she's got a bell… *(Gasps, realizing)* Bloody Hell! Unless she doesn't!

(Lights snap back up on NELLES *and* TRICITY.*)*

TRICITY: That can't have been easy. With the Vicar.

NELLES: No…though thank the bloody heavens about Lavender…

TRICITY: True. *(Pouring out more drinks)* Now. What ever are we to do—two single ladies alone in a well-stocked public house.

NELLES: Oh nonsense, you and Armitage will patch things up.

TRICITY: The sooner I can forget him, the better…He and Miss Spoon were—

NELLES: *(Guessing)* No…

TRICITY: It's why I even went and…Oh I may as well confess it. I couldn't sleep the night after the Celebration…so I went out for a stroll and before I knew it I found myself standing in the graveyard in front of that bell device, and…and…well I snipped the little wire leading down to her coffin.

NELLES: *(Aghast)* You snipped the little wire? How could you snip the little wire!

TRICITY: *(Simply)* With my little scissors.

NELLES: Oh my dear! You didn't!

TRICITY: It's not as if I murdered someone! Yes, I did it in a fit of pique, but—I mean, the Vicar did pronounce her dead after all!

NELLES: No no, you're right...

TRICITY: I mean she was dead, wasn't she?

NELLES: Of course she was! Well, I mean...surely.

TRICITY: Well...yes....so....there we are.

NELLES: Yes....there we are....

(We hear, faintly, heavy breathing, a beating heart, as BOSCH *walks backs to the graveyard, where* WICKER *is dancing miserably in place)*

BOSCH: ...there we are... There we are.... *(Calls out—)* Wicker—

WICKER: Is she coming back?!

BOSCH: Get on to Tricity's, you'll be sleeping there tonight...

(Up on a beating heart, and SPOON *is revealed inside a coffin under the ground)*

SPOON: *(Clearly weak)* ...I'm here...I'm still underneath it all...

BOSCH: But nobody knows....

SPOON: Are you who I think you are?

BOSCH: Call me Cupid.

SPOON: I know you. Fat-faced brat of a boy. Devilish quiver.

BOSCH: Deadly, even.

SPOON: Cupid, you're a menace, but you're no murderer—

BOSCH: Don't believe it.

SPOON: On the contrary, you can save me. And you want to.

BOSCH: *(Tortured)* I do want to.

SPOON: More than that, Tom. You need to. You're stuck here without me!

BOSCH: There are questions I want answered once and for all—

SPOON: You'll get the answers—just get me out!

BOSCH: *(Frustrated)* Let me think!

SPOON: Well think about this—Don't you know what's buried with me?

BOSCH: *(Nodding at sudden realization)* My History!

TOOM: Bloody Hell! Vicar! I just figgered out where your Book is!

LEAP: *(Excitedly)* You did?! Well out with it, man! Where's my History of Brood!?

TOOM: I buried it with Miss Spoon.

(Good healthy pause)

LEAP: Eh?

TOOM: I'm serious.

LEAP: Well I hope you have an explanation!

TOOM: I lent it to Miss Spoon, you see, cause she said she'd love to read it, "get to know your customers"— that's an axiom, but then the next day—

LEAP: *(Interrupting, with his new-found serenity)* You know what, Mister Stoup? Bugger explanations. A thousand explanations won't bring it back, will it.

TOOM: Ah but here's the thing, Vicar.

SPOON: *(To BOSCH)* My life is in your hands!

BOSCH: *(Growing realization)* And has been for years…
(To TOOM*)* Say it.

TOOM: What if the bell were to ring. The whole town
would come with their spades…We could open that
box, and none would be the wiser…

(Pause. LEAP *sees the worth of the plan, but the only way he
can agree is by saying—)*

LEAP: Let it be known…that I've expressly forbidden
you to go near that bell device.

TOOM: Oh aye. *("winking")* …Mind, it's been known for
a wind or a worm to trigger such a device….

LEAP: Well…then that would be out of our hands,
wouldn't it….

TOOM: It would.

LEAP: I'm glad we understand each other. I'll see you
for breakfast.

TOOM: I'll find you an egg.

SPOON: They'll open this coffin…I'll live another day…
and this nightmare will be over…!

BOSCH: *(Realization growing, to self—)* I'm beginning to
awake already—

*(*BOSCH *turns towards* TRICITY'*s room as lights up on*
TRICITY *and* WICKER*.)*

TRICITY: Time for sleep, Master Grigs. Night's arrived
and the clouds are all shaped like sheep…"a-hishi-baa"
they bleat…

WICKER: But Miss, the whole town's not really angry at
me, is it?

TRICITY: Canny noo little calf, and never you mind. Our
one chance at happiness, and you swallowed it, but
never you mind.

WICKER: It's nice to be with you, Miss. You're nice.
It's nicest of all when Mister Bosch is nice, because I
love him. Maybe if I did something nice for him... *(An
idea—)* I'll steal the strongbox! I'll bring it to Jarl van.
He'll crack the riddle in one go and then I'll be Wicker
Who Saved The Town I will.

*(BOSCH, who had been discreetly listening, begins a lullaby.
TRICITY sings to GRIGS, and they send the town to sleep)*

BOSCH: *(Singing)*
Let it all die down...die dilly, die down...

TRICITY/BOSCH: A mouse in the gutter is et by an owl
The geese are aflutter, the moon wears a scowl
A nag's on the loose, after years of abuse
And a spider is dangling from a self-woven noose...

But somewhere a snowfall in silence idyllic
Floats toward the coats of the sheep on the hillock
Peace and contentment aren't so far away
It's time for the embers to dwindle to grey...

Let it all die down
Die dilly, die dilly, die down, die down...
Send the goose round and we'll pluck it for down
For pillows for setting
Us dreaming and letting
This flame in my heart...
Die down, down, die dilly...die down....

*(LEAP, NELLES, TOOM, and finally TRICITY, blow out their
candles. The stage is now dark save for SPOON's coffin—)*

SPOON: *(Nervous)* You've shut it all out...

BOSCH: Total darkness...total silence...total stillness...
just as you requested.

SPOON: I take it back! Wait... Steady on—it's not
completely dark after all—

BOSCH: Isn't it?

SPOON: I still see…I see…. *(We see the blink of the lighthouse)* …a blink.

(We hear, faintly, a heartbeat, growing louder and more rapid as scene progresses)

BOSCH: You see yourself. What's left of you.

SPOON: It'll do. So long as I can see that dear little blink, I know I'm alive!

BOSCH: But when it goes out….so will you.

SPOON: But surely I'll be saved. The bell—

BOSCH: The bell is not for you.

SPOON: But we had an arrangement!

BOSCH: It's becoming clearer now, the tale of the last ember. "Tis a Salesman That'll Snuff It!"

(Lights up on HOOTHER, *quite agitated, standing in front of the lighthouse light)*

HOOTHER: *(To self)* Anna Livia—you've brought me to this. Up the top of the stairs to the flame—

SPOON: I won't let you!

BOSCH: You're burning on nothing!

SPOON: But Tom don't you know I'm Hetty?

BOSCH: No. No you're not!

SPOON: Don't ask me why I've denied it! But every chapter, every excuse you've spun on my behalf has come to this—I'm ready to come back now!

HOOTHER: *(To self)* To smother my very livelihood.

BOSCH: I don't want you back—

SPOON: But you've been waiting for me!

BOSCH: You're not Hetty! Hetty lived and breathed… you're just a swindling salesman—a tangled mess of memories pasted together with some lurid fiction—

HOOTHER: *(To self)* Fool! Do you think you'll end these days and then your brain ablaze will cool? I promise you—there's nothing out that door but a horribly more flammable fuel!

SPOON: Let me stay—

BOSCH: *(Pleading to* HETTY/SPOON*)* Let me go.

HOOTHER: *(Deciding to leave)* Let us go.

SPOON: I won't.

HOOTHER: No more debate.

SPOON: Wait! We were caught in the rain—

BOSCH: Don't remind me—

SPOON: We were caught in the rain—

BOSCH: You're not Hetty!

SPOON: How wet you were—

BOSCH: *(Unable to resist)* The rain dripped off that rabbity nose of yours—

SPOON: But you were wetter. You were soaked—

BOSCH: You pushed me in the lake is why!

SPOON: You didn't mind the rain after that.

BOSCH: I don't remember thanking you.

SPOON: You didn't. You pulled me into the lake with you—

BOSCH: Louse.

SPOON: Nutter.

BOSCH: Scoundrel.

SPOON: Lover.

BOSCH: I said don't remind me.

SPOON: You caught a cold—

BOSCH: You were beautiful…

SPOON: I'll always be.

BOSCH: "Stay in, it's warm," I said…

SPOON: "Let me out," I said.

BOSCH: And I did.

SPOON: *(Now intensely and urgently)* …Tom…let me out…. Let me out of—

BOSCH: *(Coming to senses, interrupting, savagely)* So you can litter my brain with bells that yield up nothing but corpses?! So you can disseminate the sham assurance that the dead never die, that memories are living things instead of the mechanical pigs they are?! So you can yet again crowd out the here-and-now with chattering ghosts?! *(With unrebuttable resolve)* No, it's you or the boy. I choose the boy. Now say your goodbyes to the world.

SPOON: *(Still desperate)* The leaves underfoot—

HOOTHER: Last volume—

SPOON: *(More wistful)* …or hand clasped in another—

HOOTHER: Last folio—

SPOON: *(More resigned to fate)* Or wondering what's for dinner—

HOOTHER: Last appendix—

SPOON: Last words—

HOOTHER: Last word—

SPOON: last breath—

HOOTHER: *(Preparing to blow out lamp)* One breath is all it takes—

SPOON: All else I leave unspoken, unthought, undone—

HOOTHER: You're done.

SPOON: Undone.

HOOTHER: No more.

SPOON: Be sure of it.

HOOTHER: Done…

SPOON: …yes…

HOOTHER: Done.

(Beat, and then—)

BOSCH: *(With intensity)* Snuff it!

*(*HOOTHER *blows out the lighthouse blink with one breath. Heartbeat ceases. Darkness)*

BOSCH: *(Softly to self, realization growing)* …silence…but there are no dead silences for those still in the world… only pregnant pauses…all ready to give birth to still more commotion and clamour…and music…I've been slumbering in this town too long I think… Now wake us up!

(The bell device begins ringing like mad. LEAP, NELLES, TRICITY *start from their sleep.* WICKER, *with strongbox, runs toward the grave, and is stopped by* BOSCH.)

BOSCH: Where do you think you're going.

WICKER: To the grave of course.

BOSCH: *(Firmly, looking into his eyes)* No you're not.

WICKER: But—

BOSCH: Let it go, Wicker.

WICKER: But maybe—

BOSCH: Let it go….Let it go…

*(*WICKER *suddenly breaks down—a different sort of weeping than we've seen—the release of nine years of sadness and guilt. He clutches* BOSCH *as if his life depended on it.* BOSCH *holds* WICKER, *and, through tears, as the bell continues ringing—)*

BOSCH: ...but what was it you said... *(Gaining strength)* "You can take everything I have...but still I'll remember the music..."!

(And at that, flags suddenly rise on the device, and the ringing transmutes to an even louder bleating blaring alarm; then, underneath, the rattle of military drums, and the siren transmutes into a solemn, stirring melody played on a hundred bagpipes. LEAP, NELLES, and TOOM, in a dazed procession, make their way to the grave and freeze as the music fades.)

BOSCH: They unearthed the coffin, and buried it again. And Vicar Leap reclaimed his History, Toom the Stoup mouthed a vow of repentance, and Mrs Nelles said she didn't know what she was thinking—depriving the town of the "water of life" for so long—and invited all of Brood back for a sorely-needed drink.

(Lights down on all except WICKER and BOSCH. WICKER is holding the strongbox)

BOSCH: And that leaves us.

(BOSCH removes the poorbox effortlessly from WICKER's hand.)

WICKER: I don't want to be in Brood anymore. I want to leave.

BOSCH: *(Coyly)* What we're needing I'm thinking is the strongbox.

WICKER: I have the strongbox! I was going to bring it to Hoother—but the light's out!

BOSCH: Oh yes—

(We see HOOTHER and TRICITY—puppets?—in tableau.)

BOSCH: Jarl van Hoother sat snug as could be

Until he decided—

HOOTHER: "I'm sick of my tea."

BOSCH: So employing the oil he opened his door
But the blast of the draught had him shook to the core
And he fell with a flop, and there he'd have stayed

TRICITY: "If a pretty young maid hadn't come to his aid…"

(We hear a harpsichord, and see bow and curtsy)

BOSCH:
And you'll find in more than one poem it's written
That out of the blue, two hearts can be smitten

(We hear a firing of two arrows)

HOOTHER: "And I'll teach you of snails,
and of owls, and their beaks—"

TRICITY: "And I'll teach you still more,
when you take off those breeks…."

BOSCH: And fifty-three children they sired and raised
And their days left them dazed…and agrin…and
  amazed…

(We see the puppets of HOOTHER *and* TRICITY *hold hands
and go off together.)*

BOSCH: And so you see, we don't need to be bothering
him with any strongbox.

WICKER: But we don't know the word.

BOSCH: Oh yes we do. "And with one simple magic
word, Tom Chimney Bosch saved the day, and he
took the hand of his young charge and off they
scramooshed, to catch a ship to new and pleasanter
ports."

WICKER: So what's the word.

BOSCH: "I'm dead, yet alive." That means it's Latin, a
dead language, yet still about.

WICKER: But what is it.

BOSCH: "It's the cause of sadness and the vanquisher of sadness."

WICKER: But what is it.

BOSCH: "It's often difficult to say, and difficult to hear."

WICKER: But what is it.

BOSCH: "When it appears, nothing stays the same."

WICKER: So open it! Please, Mister Bosch, I want us to leave Brood once and for all!

BOSCH: And so we will. With the only word that will let us. *(And he turns the dials on the box—)*

F...I...N...I...S

(As BOSCH *turns the dials, the word, one letter at a time, appear [projected?]. We hear a loud click of a latch, the lid opens, music pours out.* BOSCH *takes* WICKER's *hand, and they exit together as lights dim briskly to black, leaving only the "FINIS" projection illuminated.)*

END OF PLAY

AN EXTRA SONG—

(While sitting at the fire at the top of the show, before his first lines, BOSCH has the option of playing the accordion or concertina while singing the below.)

BOSCH: You replaced my eyes with a leaking pump
T'wasn't very nice…
You replaced my heart with a burning coal
I'd rather it was ice…
You then traded my brain for a nest of wasps
And it stings
Oh Christ,
There's little I can call my own…my own…
I'll be down to a tooth if you don't leave me alone….

You traded my bones for some broken sticks
Now it's hard to stand…
You switched my hide with a long-dead cow's
Now I bear your brand…
Then a wheezing bellows became my lungs,
And Can I breathe?
Oh Man…
There's little I can call my own…my own…
I'll be down to a tooth if you don't leave me alone…

And gratitude you'll
Nae hear from me ghoul
Behold—I'm a scrap heap
The arse of a mule!

But I won't let you win, you can flatter…cajole
I know that I'm gone if I give you my soul….
But.

You'll replace my blood with nettle soup
And upon my life
You'll take my voice and I'll do with the squeak
Of a broken fife
You'll supplant every part of me, bit by bit
But will you ever be
my wife…?

There's little I can call my own…my own…
But if you are gone…blast it…leave me alone…
What's left of me…won't you…leave…alone….